PUFFIN BOOKS

Editor: Kaye Webb

THE MYSTERY OF THE CROSS-EYED MAN

IT was the beginning of the summer holidays, and Daniel was alone in Paris, in charge of his small brother Manou. They were due to meet their parents the next day from Philadelphia, and then to travel to Chiberta, near Biarritz, where their grandfather was planning a mass family reunion at his new villa.

It was all supposed to be very simple, because Grandfather was an organizing genius. He had given the family their 'marching orders', detailed instructions of what trains to catch, where to stay the night, etc., weeks in advance, and his plans *always* worked like clockwork. But this time things went wrong. Daniel and Manou's parents couldn't get to Paris because of a train strike and one of the uncles was in a car crash.

It was beastly on their own in the hotel, so Daniel decided he would get Manou to Chiberta on his own. It meant hitchhiking (there were still no trains and their money had been stolen), and a sinister cross-eyed man followed them wherever they went. Two other boys had run away from home, and the hunt was up . . .

Paul Berna has two other books published in Puffins: *A Hundred Million Francs* and *Flood Warning*. He is most recommended to readers who enjoy 'almost grown-up' adventure stories.

PAUL BERNA

The Mystery of the Cross-eyed Man

Translated from the French by
JOHN BUCHANAN-BROWN

Illustrated by
BARRY WILKINSON

PUFFIN BOOKS
in association with The Bodley Head

Puffin Books, Penguin Books Ltd, Harmondsworth,
Middlesex, England
Penguin Books, 625 Madison Avenue,
New York, New York 10022, U.S.A.
Penguin Books Australia Ltd, Ringwood,
Victoria, Australia
Penguin Books Canada Ltd, 2801 John Street,
Markham, Ontario, Canada L3R 1B4
Penguin Books (N.Z.) Ltd, 182-190
Wairau Road, Auckland 10, New Zealand

Les Pèlerins de Chiberta first published in France 1958
This translation first published in Great Britain by The Bodley Head 1965
Published in Puffin Books 1968
Reprinted 1977

Made and printed in Great Britain by
Richard Clay (The Chaucer Press) Ltd,
Bungay, Suffolk
Set in Monotype Imprint

Contents

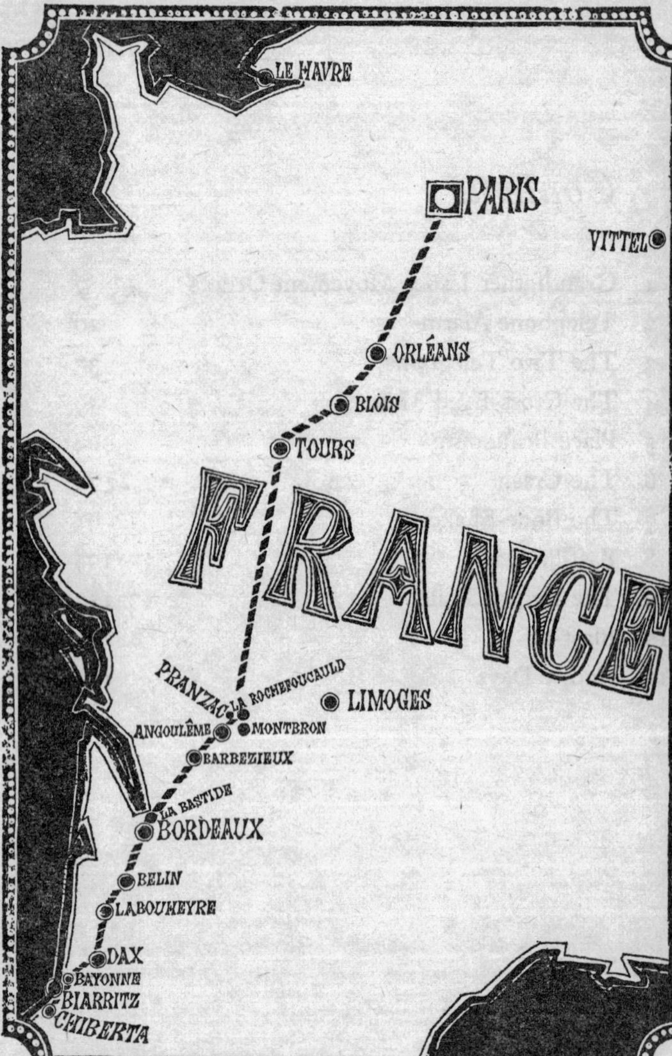

LE HAVRE
PARIS
VITTEL
ORLÉANS
BLOIS
TOURS
FRANCE
PRANZAC
LA ROCHEFOUCAULD
LIMOGES
ANGOULÊME
MONTBRON
BARBEZIEUX
LA BASTIDE
BORDEAUX
BELIN
LABOUHEYRE
DAX
BAYONNE
BIARRITZ
CHIBERTA

I

Grandfather Issues Movement Orders

DANIEL and Manou faced one another across the table in the smart green and white dining-room of the Hotel Regina. At nearby tables other hotel-guests turned to cast friendly glances at the tall fourteen-year-old, with his hair so carefully brushed and in his best clothes, and at the fair-haired little boy opposite him enjoying a large slice of raspberry tart. Over-awed by the atmosphere of the luxury hotel, and realizing that they were the centre of interest, the two boys were on their best behaviour and Daniel was watching Manou with almost motherly care.

The head-waiter came up to their table and leaned towards Daniel with a smile on his face.

'Would the gentleman like a little more tart?' he asked, and his eyes flickered towards Manou.

Daniel looked at his young brother. He was prepared to spoil him, if only to ensure his good behaviour.

'Like some more? Half a slice?'

'No thanks!' The gentleman puffed a bit as he answered. 'But I should like to have five or six lettuce leaves wrapped up in a piece of paper, if I might, please?'

'It's for Patapon,' Daniel explained to the head-waiter.

As he spoke he lifted the corner of the table-cloth which was draped over the seat of an empty chair. The head-waiter's eyebrows shot up when he saw, sitting in a bird-cage, a fat, rat-like creature with glistening little black eyes, silken muzzle, and white and reddish-brown whiskers.

Patapon squeaked and ran round his cage.

'He's mine!' Manou explained proudly. 'Granny gave

him to me for Easter. He comes when I call him, he can sit up and beg and he sleeps in my bed with me.'

'I'll see that Patapon gets his lettuce,' the head-waiter said with a respectful bow. 'I'll have it prepared for him at once. Where would he like it?'

'In our room,' Manou answered. 'If I let him out in here, all the ladies will be climbing up on their chairs.'

All three laughed conspiratorially.

'Would you like me to keep this table for you tomorrow?' the head-waiter asked.

'No, thank you.' Daniel still smiled. 'It won't be big enough then. There'll be four of us tomorrow, and six the day after.'

'And the day after that?' Manou asked, his blue eyes gleaming with excitement.

'In three days' time I expect we'll all be at Chiberta,' Daniel finished.

'A pleasant spot,' said the head-waiter. 'I worked at the Country Club for a couple of seasons. Where will you gentlemen be staying?'

'With our grandfather, at the Villa Etchola,' Daniel explained. 'It's a big place built in the Basque style, with a huge garden. He bought it at the end of last year.'

The head-waiter whistled softly.

'I know it well,' he said. 'The villa's at the end of the lake by the golf-course. You'll have a good time, it's a lovely place.'

Chiberta! Daniel still only knew it as a name and a few measurements which his grandfather had sent in a letter to him at school at Besançon. But that had been enough to give substance to his dreams of the holidays, dreams which come to every schoolboy's mind as he sits hunched over the textbooks he would like to see burned. Manou had had the good luck to spend the first five months of the year at Chiberta, but he was too young to be able to paint a picture of the place for his older brother in really attractive colours. His one concern had been the safety and comfort of the furry little creature of which he was so fond.

And now they were on their way to Chiberta. Daniel felt quite happy about the first stage of their journey.

Up to now he had scrupulously adhered to the time-table his grandfather had so meticulously drawn up for them. Nothing had gone wrong and there seemed no likelihood of any mishaps in the future.

Old Monsieur Quint had an amiable eccentricity – he always enjoyed organizing, and would never let his nearest and dearest set out on a journey without a string of warnings and instructions which he pompously called his 'movement orders'. Not even his grown-up sons – Daniel's father and his uncles, Jérôme and Jules – could go without them. Because of his temporary responsibilities Daniel, too, had been given his 'movement orders'. They comprised a foolscap sheet of squared paper on which everything had been noted in the smallest detail in the old man's tiny, close, but clear handwriting.

For at least the third time during the meal Daniel produced his wallet, gravely opened it in front of little Manou and read, with secret amusement, his 'orders'.

Vittel. *Reach the station ten minutes before the train leaves – that is at 10:10 a.m. Give the driver of the hotel taxi a 2-franc tip for his kindness. Keep hold of Manou's hand and go to the platform shown on the departure board. Get into a first-class coach marked* – Vittel-Paris. *It would be best for you to take the two corner seats on the corridor side of your compartment. Keep a tactful eye on Manou and take firm measures if he misbehaves. Hold his hand whenever he wants to use the toilet.* (He had – at least twenty times, just for the fun of stretching his legs and showing Patapon to the neighbouring compartments.) *Ask the dining-car attendant for two tickets for the first sitting, and wait until he comes by ringing his bell before you go to the dining-car.* (It had been one mad rush, but Daniel and Manou had managed to beat everyone in the hundred yards' race up the corridor.) *See that Manou does not eat too much.* (That had been no easy task with an appetite and a persistence like Manou's.) *Spend the rest of the journey reading or playing sensible games, and do not pester the other passengers with your chatter.* Paris. *The train should get into the Gare de l'Est at 4:15 p.m. Don't leave anything in the compartment and keep tight hold of Manou's hand as you pass the barrier. Take a taxi to the Hotel Régina, 124 Avenue Marceau, where three adjoining rooms have been reserved for the family (Nos. 615, 616 and 617). Go up to Room 617 where a small bed has been put up for Manou. Wash your face and hands. Keep an eye on Manou and the taps! Rest for at least an hour before dinner. In no circumstances are you to go out of the hotel and roam the streets. Go down to the hotel restaurant at 7:30 p.m. and don't over-eat. Menu: soup, grill, green vegetables, fruit and a small pastry for Manou, if he has been good . . .*

At that very moment Manou was finishing his huge slice of tart, and Daniel thought to himself that, all things considered, his young brother had well deserved it. Naturally Grandfather's 'movement orders' had taken everything into account, everything, that is, except the presence of Patapon, who was in some respects outside the old gentleman's authority. Patapon himself was a splendid white and russet guinea-pig which Grandmother had been misguided enough to give to Manou some three months before as a reward for a whole week's exemplary good behaviour. Manou had been thrilled with his pet, had christened it Patapon, cuddled it like a doll, fed it regularly and would not move a step without the birdcage in which his pet had just enough room to turn round. Of course Patapon had had to come on the trip and Daniel had had a struggle to stop his young brother creating chaos on the train with the guinea-pig. No sooner had they started than the old lady sitting next to Manou had screeched like a pea-hen when she found Patapon climbing up her arm to nestle familiarly on her shoulder. Daniel had to apologize hurriedly to the lady and lock the escaper in his cage, threatening Manou with no pudding for the rest of his life and a full report to Grandfather.

After this, all was comparatively quiet until they reached Paris. At the hotel, Patapon sniffed inquisitively round the skirting-board of Room 617, explored the bathroom attached to it and then went unconcernedly to sleep in a dip in one of the pillows. When the time came for them to go downstairs a tremendous argument took place between the two brothers on the advisability of appearing in the restaurant with the creature in tow, and Daniel had only just managed to insist that Patapon should be kept in his cage. 'Only just', however, meant giving way on the 'small pastry' Grandfather had left to his discretion.

As soon as dinner was over, Daniel took his young brother by the hand and the two boys went quietly up to Room 617. Patapon scuttled two or three times round the room as soon as he was let out of his cage and then buried his face in the lettuce leaves.

'I'm very cross about Chiberta,' Manou said seriously as he undressed. 'The villas nearby seem to be full of cats. I'll have to keep my eyes open. That big black tom from the Villa Ramuntcho's always in our garden. If he meets my little Patapon one day, he'll swallow him in one mouthful.'

'Put him on a lead,' Daniel answered sharply. 'Then you won't have to worry. That's what I should have done with you when we left Vittel this morning. A good strong piece of rope round your neck would have saved me a lot of bother.'

The idea appealed to Manou and he burst out laughing. Daniel seized him in a bear-hug, dumped him under the hot shower, dried him carefully and put him to bed. *Don't forget to make Manou say his prayers*, Grandfather's orders had read. This the cherubic Manou was only too ready to do, kneeling beside his bed, clutching Patapon. Then his elder brother tucked him up carefully.

'Go to sleep now,' Daniel said gently. 'A good old snooze until tomorrow morning . . .'

'Of course I shall, but you must tell me a story first. Granny always does.'

Daniel could not help smiling. Standing orders had also laid down, *Tell Manou a story to help him go to sleep.* So, without overstraining his imagination, he began:

'Once upon a time there was a little boy called Manou, who decided to go on a long journey with his best friend, a sort of small-scale pig called Patapon.'

Manou seemed to like the way the story began. Once he heard his name mentioned he had to go on listening.

'At first everything went well,' Daniel continued. 'Manou had thirty gold pieces in his purse, so he wanted for nothing and did not quibble about the lettuce-hearts that the greedy Patapon gobbled up at every meal. Then, oh goodness me, they were going through a big city when the stupid Manou lost his purse! After that there were no more good meals and comfortable hotels for them! Instead of travelling in luxury, the silly pair had to take to the road like a couple of tramps. All sorts of people chased them. Some shouted, "Where did you steal that fine guinea-pig?" Others called to Manou, "You're too small to be tramping the roads. Go home at once or we'll send for the police!" And so they had the police after them. Luckily Manou could run very fast indeed. And anyway he was so small that every night he could curl up in a rabbit hole to go to sleep with his Patapon. All the same, they had to cover twenty-five miles a day over rough roads and pot-holes and that wears your feet out. Patapon's were the first to go. First his front paws wore out and then his back ones . . .'

'You're not joking?' asked an open-mouthed Manou. 'What happened then?'

'On the fifth day,' Daniel went on, 'Manou had to take Patapon on his back and walk on, carrying that great fat lump who could think of nothing but eating lettuce, drinking and sleeping, and never did anything to help. In a few days' time, Manou was as thin as a rake because he had had nothing to eat. Patapon, however, was getting fatter and heavier. "There's not much point in going on like this," Manou said to himself and threw his guinea-pig into a ditch. "If I go a step farther I'll drop down dead. Let's leave Patapon where he is to look after himself." Patapon was frightened. "Don't do that," he cried, "my paws haven't grown again! The first cat that comes along will think I'm a rat and make mincemeat of me!" Manou licked his lips. "All right," he said. "Since you're afraid of being left behind to die, I'll eat you myself. It'll do me good and you'll stay in the family that way!"'

'How horrid!' Manou shouted, and hid his head under the bed-clothes.

As a result, Daniel, who inclined towards spit-roasting Patapon, had to alter his plot.

'Fortunately,' he said, 'Manou was kind-hearted. He loved his little Patapon far too much to do a thing like that. By not walking so far and resting for longer periods he was able to finish his journey without getting caught and without dropping his burden. In fact, when they arrived, Patapon was sleek and plump and his new paws had grown an inch at least.'

'And where did they arrive anyway?' asked a sleepy little voice.

'At Chiberta,' Daniel replied, saying the first name that came into his head.

'And is it really a true story?' Manou asked again, hardly able to keep his eyes open.

'It could happen,' Daniel said, without another thought. 'Anyway, let it be a warning to you never to go out into the woods alone with your Patapon. . . . And now, go to sleep.'

'But you haven't kissed Patapon good-night!' Manou suddenly exclaimed, sitting up in bed.

Daniel shrugged.

'You make me sick. Catch me kissing that dirty little beast on the side of the nose! Don't be so silly.'

'Dirty little beast!' Manou shrieked. 'Kiss him at once and say sorry to him, or I won't go to sleep.'

Then he burst into tears. It infuriated Daniel, but he had to give way to avoid further trouble. Muttering under his breath, he kissed Patapon and tucked his young tyrant of a brother into bed once more. Five minutes later Manou was fast asleep.

Daniel switched off the ceiling light and got into bed. He glanced for a moment at his young brother, peacefully asleep in the darkest corner of the room. The shutters were closed but the long July twilight filtered through as though into some cave beneath the waves, full of promise for the fine days to come at Chiberta. Daniel listened. The hotel was wrapped in the silence of its fitted carpets, but around him and Manou he could feel the big city alive with its subdued rumble and grumble. Suddenly he felt very lonely. But a story like the one he had told Manou could never happen. Besides, Daniel's task, despite his strong sense of responsibility, was merely to take charge of one pleasant stage of their journey to Chiberta. All had been planned ahead, and despite a last-minute alteration of a minor detail, nothing could upset the superb scheme Grandfather had drawn up.

Monsieur Quint was an organizing genius, and he prided himself on using any situation to his own advantage, no matter how involved it might appear to be. Towards the end of the previous year, he had sold up his business, disposed of his house in Bordeaux and bought the splendid villa which he had long coveted as a place in which to spend his retirement. He had moved in in January with Granny, their daughter-in-law and little Manou, who was just five, and had then determined to hold a reunion of his scattered family. He had three sons: Daniel's and Manou's father, Pascal, covered the Americas for a large firm of public works contractors; Jérôme, a bachelor, ran an import-export agency in Libreville, in the French Congo; and the youngest, Jules, worked for a car-manufacturer in Turin. After months of writing to and fro to get each to agree in principle to the scheme, all three were sent 'movement orders' which were models of their kind, arranging dates, routes, means of transport and hotels, and finishing with the general instruction, '*Everyone is to be at Chiberta on 15 July: not a day sooner, and, if possible, not a day later.*'

Monsieur Quint had even drawn an operations map for this family reunion which he proudly showed to Daniel. Each little movement of the Quint forces was detailed and marked off as soon as it had been completed.

Things started to move at the end of February, when Daniel's and Manou's mother, Lucy Quint, went off to rejoin her husband who was then in Philadelphia. She left her younger son with her in-laws, promising to bring his father back in time, and berths were booked for them on the *Armoric*, due to dock at Le Havre on the morning of 11 July.

Towards the middle of June, Monsieur Quint shut up the Villa Etchola and went to Vittel to take the cure, Granny and little Manou going with him. They planned to leave there for Paris on 10 July, so as to meet Pascal Quint and his wife from the boat-train. They would stay at the Hotel Régina for a day or two, and then this first group would go straight back to Chiberta on the Paris–Biarritz express on 15 July. There they would find Uncle Jérôme who would have landed the night before at Bordeaux from the West African liner, the *Président Dupas*.

Five days earlier, Uncle Jules was due to have set off by car from Turin with his wife Elvisa and their two small children. He planned to cross the South of France in easy stages, camping wherever he could in the luxury caravan he had hired for the purpose. Thus he was the only one who had to think of keeping to a schedule and of arriving at the front door of the villa amid the cheers of the rest of the family.

Finally, Daniel himself, away at his boarding-school at Besançon, had had his 'movement orders' at the very beginning of June. '*The estimable Father Froment has just written to tell me*,' Grandfather himself had written, '*that the doors of your prison house open on 5 July, an exceedingly convenient date. As you are used to travelling by yourself, you will arrange to take the first available train to Vittel and join us in full marching order*.'

When the day came, Daniel was very happy to be once more with his grandparents and his young brother, Manou, in the green garden of the Hotel Rosaria.

Unfortunately, however, only twenty-four hours before they were due to set out for Paris, Grandfather's beautiful plans began to disintegrate. Although Monsieur and Madame Quint had finished their cure, it was essential for them to have one last consultation with their doctor before they left Vittel. Now, as it happened, the latter had to go away at that very point for two days to attend the funeral of one of his relations. Monsieur Quint made a great fuss of his own health and that of Granny, and so he decided to stay on for two more days even if it meant breaking the arrangement to meet the passengers from the *Armoric*.

Granny was most upset at the thought of the latter arriving in Paris after being away for so long and having neither parents nor children there to greet them.

'Why don't we send Daniel and Manou on ahead?' she had suggested to Grandfather. 'It's not far by train, and there are through carriages from here. Daniel's a sensible boy and he'll take good care of his little brother. They'll only have one night on their own at the Régina, and the next morning they can be on the platform of the Gare Saint-Lazare to meet their parents. Pascal and Lucy will be thrilled to see them and won't be so disappointed at having to wait until the next day before we arrive.'

Grandfather stared at Daniel over the top of his glasses.

'I'll draw up your "movement orders",' he told him gravely, 'and then all you have to do is exactly what I tell you.'

That same day he telephoned the Hotel Régina to warn them that the children would be arriving on their own, and then he arranged for the heavy luggage to be sent off in advance to Chiberta. The pace was increasing, the family reunion was entering its most hectic stage, and Daniel was sure that the genial organizing spirit behind it all was not displeased by these additional complications.

Daniel's share in the game was nearly over, and just before he went to sleep he picked up his 'movement orders' once more and re-read their closing lines: '*Get up at eight o'clock precisely. Ring for room-service and order two breakfasts, with coffee for you and chocolate for Manou. Wash thoroughly and dress carefully. Be particularly careful that Manou does not put his trousers on back-to-front. At half-past-ten ask the hall-porter at the hotel to get you a taxi and drive to the Arrival platforms at the Gare Saint-Lazare. Buy a nice bunch of red roses for Mummy (there are two florists' shops near the waiting-room). Manou is to carry the flowers and you are both to go to the platform at which the boat-train is shown; it is due in at eleven-fifteen. When your parents arrive, hand over to your Father the fat brown envelope containing his mail, his business papers, some French money (of which he is sure to be short) and his movement orders setting out my instructions for the time he is to wait for me.'*

There ended the part Daniel had to play. He folded the paper and gave a deep sigh. All that day he had enjoyed, in his own way, the flavour of his brief independence and of the thousand and one small responsibilities which Manou's presence imposed on him. He had got a lot of pleasure out of this and out of impressing his younger brother with his command of an unusual situation. But tomorrow all would return to its accustomed routine. Daniel would have nothing to worry about. It was a pity. He would have liked so much to have had the anxiety of looking after the brat for a little longer and of showing him that a boy of fourteen, faced with the pressures of modern life, could act like a man.

2

Telephone Alarm

THE morning sun was already hot as it poured through the window of Room 617 from which there was a splendid view of the centre of Paris and the leafy banks of the Seine. Daniel whistled cheerfully as he got his younger brother ready for the moment that was approaching. At ten-twenty-five he gave his own hair one last flick of the comb and then he walked slowly round Manou examining him from top to toe with all the care of a sergeant-major inspecting the guard.

'You'll do.' He was satisfied. 'Smart as paint.'

'May I take Patapon with me?' Manou asked.

'No!' barked Daniel, determined on a show of authority. 'We're not humping that bird-cage all the way to the station. Mummy and Daddy would be simply furious. They can meet your guinea-pig a bit later on. Let's go downstairs now, and mind you behave yourself.'

As he stepped out of the lift, holding Manou by the hand, he noticed a crowd of worried-looking guests round the reception-desk. The telephone-booths were the centre of a seething scrum, and groups of people were talking loudly in the foyer, their voices mingling in an incomprehensible hubbub. This did not alarm Daniel, for the anxious bustle seemed to him a normal part of the hectic life of Paris. There was not a page-boy or porter in sight, so they had to go out into the sun-drenched street in search of a taxi.

'It'll give us a breath of fresh air,' Daniel said. 'We've plenty of time anyway.'

The two boys set off at a good pace, but they had to go nearly to the Étoile before they found a taxi. The driver did not say a word as he pulled down the flag on the meter, but he gave the youngsters an odd look when he heard where they wanted to go. Daniel took no notice at the time; he was far too happy at the thought of seeing his parents again.

It was only when, less than ten minutes later, they reached the Gare Saint-Lazare that he felt a twinge of anxiety. On the pavements outside the arrival and departure platforms was a mournful crowd of people, standing still as if stupefied. It took Daniel all his time to force his way through to the waiting-room. A few suburban trains had just pulled in, and numbers of discontented passengers were slowly filtering away along passages and subways. People burdened with parcels and squalling infants stood and gazed at the closed barriers.

Little Manou pranced coltishly in tow as his elder brother wormed his way through the crowd. Daniel thought the roses in the florist's neither fine nor fresh enough, and he chose instead a bunch of Parma violets, elegantly haloed with lace-paper.

'Hold them properly, not upside down,' he said as he gave them to Manou. 'It's a bouquet, you know, not a cabbage.'

The florist smiled at the two boys who had just bought a bunch of flowers for their mother.

'We're waiting for the train from Le Havre – the boat-train,' Daniel said, very pleased with himself, as they were leaving the shop.

'Well, you've still some slight hope, young man.' The woman sighed and shook her head. 'Of course no trains are going out, but one or two are still coming in.'

'What did you say?' Daniel gasped.

'Rail strike. Started at eight this morning all over the country,' the florist went on. 'Didn't you know about it?'

Daniel stood shocked: Grandfather's plan continued to go awry.

'The trains from Dieppe and Rouen came in as usual,' the florist concluded in an attempt to reassure him. 'The Le Havre train may possibly get through. Go along to Platform 12; one of the station staff may be able to tell you something.'

Little Manou only half heard this conversation, but Daniel looked so downcast that instinctively he tightened his hold on his brother's hand. This simple reminder stopped Daniel from giving way to panic. There was still a glimmer of hope.

They made their way to Platform 12. A crowd of about two hundred people pressed against the tightly shut bar-

rier. The station clock said eleven-ten, but the boat-train was not even listed on the arrival indicator. Nobody knew anything, and the station staff were evasive.

'Right!' said Daniel. 'We'll do what everyone else is doing – we'll wait for a bit. It would be silly if that wretched train sneaked in and there was nobody here to welcome Mummy and Daddy. . . . You hungry, Manou?'

'Not yet. But I shall be soon.'

'Well, when you feel your stomach flapping, we'll go back to the hotel,' Daniel promised.

In the waiting-room, people squeezed up on a seat so that they could perch on the end. They sat down side by side, hand in hand. The first fifteen minutes sped by, and they both found it rather fun to watch what was going on in the station. Once he had got over the initial shock, Daniel's spirits soon rose. There was no point in getting all worked up over a few hours' delay. The main thing was to take care of Manou and to see that he kept cheerful. The little boy still clutched his bunch of flowers, which their neighbours openly admired.

Noon came, and with it gloom settled on the drifting crowd still hopelessly remaining in the station, despite the notices at every platform – *Rail Strike: Closed Until Further Notice*. The travellers sitting beside Daniel talked despairingly among themselves, and then went off one by one, grumbling and swearing, until soon the two boys had the seat to themselves and faced a desperately empty platform. The crowd was ebbing away now, slowly, in rebelliously muttering little groups. The telephone booths were still packed solid, besieged by a heaving mob.

Daniel glanced at his watch – half-past twelve.

'I'm hungry.' Manou's voice was plaintive. 'Where's Mummy and Daddy?'

'They'll be in a little later,' Daniel answered with forced cheerfulness. 'We'll come back to the station this afternoon. We'd better have some lunch now. And Patapon's waiting for us in the hotel.'

Out of the corner of his eye he could read the disappointment on his brother's face and he feared he would see signs of worse. But Manou took it in his stride and slid off the seat. They made for the exit, leaving the empty platforms and abandoning the bunch of violets forgotten on the seat.

Outside there was a battle for taxis, but Daniel soon found a bus going to the Étoile.

'In you get,' he said as he hoisted Manou on to the rear platform, 'this will be much more fun.'

He had his own pocket-money as well as the funds Grandfather had given him in case of emergency. Together they came to a useful sum, but it was better to take care of it in case there were harder times ahead. The fickle

Manou was obviously delighted by the short bus-ride. All the same there was the trace of some slight anxiety in his expression.

'What'll happen if Mummy and Daddy don't come?' he said, and his face suddenly dissolved in alarm.

Daniel reassured him; he had already considered this question.

'Don't you worry about that. Anyway, Granny and Grandfather'll be here tomorrow evening, so we'll only be on our own for one more day.'

'But if the trains aren't running?' Manou went on with disconcerting logic.

'Oh, they'll find a coach or a car to bring them to Paris. When there's a strike they've got everything ready to keep people moving.'

In the foyer of the Régina the atmosphere of disaster was even stronger than it had been earlier that day, for a large proportion of the hotel guests were foreign tourists. It astonished Daniel that grown-ups should behave with so little self-control when things went wrong. He himself had the care of one small boy and his age was a serious handicap; yet as time went on he was learning to regard events more and more philosophically.

The manager of the Régina was a tall man in morning dress with greying hair and friendly face. He now went from group to group, advising, informing and reassuring in three languages. When he saw the two boys, he gave them a warm smile. The first thing he said confirmed the chance remarks that Daniel had made a few minutes before, less to console little Manou than to keep up his own courage.

'The passengers from the *Armoric* left Le Havre at eleven o'clock by road,' Monsieur Hébert told them as he stroked Manou's well-brushed hair. 'Don't worry, the first coaches should reach Paris at about three or four this afternoon, so your parents are sure to arrive in time for dinner. Happy now?'

Daniel's and Manou's eyes shone as they looked at one another. The pinch of anxiety that flavoured this delayed arrival only made even more delightful the thought of seeing their parents again, and Mummy and Daddy seemed twice as dear to them for having gone through the same fears.

'We'll have some lunch and then go up to our room to wait for them,' Daniel told the kindly manager.

'You are model children!' Monsieur Hébert laughed. 'Don't be afraid if you hear a knock at your door – it won't be anything alarming!'

There was nothing in Grandfather's 'movement orders' about this extra lunch and, in the circumstances, Daniel decided that they could give themselves a treat. So the two brothers ordered roast chicken with an alacrity that made their neighbours smile. The head-waiter was only too glad to give his young customers extra attention, since they had brought the gloomy dining-room back to life and gaiety. All the same, when they came to the sweet – a rainbow of ice-cream drowned in *crème chantilly* – Manou suddenly started to cry.

'The f . . . f . . . flowers!' he hiccupped through his sobs. 'I left the f . . . f . . . flowers in the st . . . st . . . station.'

Daniel turned on him.

'Stop snivelling!' he hissed. 'Everybody's looking at us. You'll make them think I bully you. I'll buy a bunch of roses from the florist in the foyer. We'll take it up to our room and then you can give it to Mummy.'

'Promise!' Manou insisted. He had set his heart on the presentation.

'Cross my heart!'

The roses in the Hotel Régina were very expensive, but Daniel was not yet old enough to question the price of his generosity. Manou went up to Room 617 with a bunch worthy of a queen – and two lettuce-hearts for his beloved Patapon. Organization was needed to suppress boredom during the hours of waiting. Daniel lowered the blinds and disposed of Manou by sending him to bed with his guinea-pig. Then he took up his watch on the narrow balcony overlooking the avenue.

Between two and four o'clock a succession of chromium-plated coaches drew up at the pavement outside the hotel and a flood of tourists emerged. It was hard to pick out individual faces in the crowd from that height, and each time Daniel, wild with impatience, went back into the room to listen for the tap on the door which never came.

Manou woke up at four o'clock, perfectly all right. The roast chicken was a thing of the past.

'I want my tea,' he said in tones that brooked no argument.

Daniel ordered a well-filled tray, from which he took only one small wafer biscuit. He nibbled this as he watched his younger brother eat. A renewal of his anxiety had taken away his appetite.

By five o'clock, nobody had knocked at the door of Room 617. A cheerful, well-fed Manou chased Patapon round the room, his war-whoops mingling with the joyous squeaks of the guinea-pig. Daniel could have screamed with frustration. He caught the youngster in full flight, went down on one knee and looked him full in the face.

'I've got to go downstairs for five minutes to talk to Monsieur Hébert. Now you be good. Stay in this room and don't touch the taps in the bathroom! I've enough to think about already without you adding to my troubles by playing the fool. . . . You understand, don't you?'

Manou was touched by the expression on his brother's

face. He nodded obediently and snuggled down in the big armchair, hugging Patapon.

'I shan't move,' he whispered, 'but do be quick.'

Daniel discovered Monsieur Hébert in a little office leading off the reception desk.

'I just can't understand it!' the manager exclaimed without giving Daniel a chance to open his mouth. 'Several passengers from the *Armoric* booked in at the hotel at about three. Others should have followed them a few minutes later. The North America Line let them have five coaches and they drove up to Paris in convoy .... Your parents must have decided at the last minute to spend the day at Le Havre.'

He seemed somewhat put out. Daniel was even more so.

'If that's what's happened,' the boy stammered, 'I'm sure Mummy and Daddy would have telephoned the hotel.'

'Possibly, but I shouldn't count on that. The long-distance lines have been jammed with calls all day. Five hours to get through to Lyons. Never known anything like it!'

Then he noticed the look of consternation on Daniel's face.

'Come on, cheer up! You're quite safe at the Régina, that's the main thing. Everyone's been kind to you, haven't they? Splendid! Then you'll have to be patient and not upset yourself by worrying any more. Good gracious, you're on holiday now!'

Daniel smiled as he thought of Chiberta as he had imagined it, with the green of the golf-course, the glassy stillness of the lake and the sparkle of the villas scattered in the pine-woods. Partly consoled, he went upstairs. Manou had not moved, but the frown on his face was menacing.

'I want to go for a walk,' he announced, 'and I want to take Patapon with me!'

Grandfather's 'movement orders' had been quite firm on this point: '*In no circumstances are you to go outside the hotel*', but Daniel decided to ignore them since they took no account of the strike. It would have driven any normal person mad to stay cooped up between four walls for another couple of hours. Patapon was put into his cage and the two brothers ran out of Room 617, intoxicated by the thought of a breath of fresh air. At the hotel entrance, Daniel told the gold-braided hall-porter that they were going out.

'We're just going to take a stroll by the river. We'll be back by seven o'clock.'

They walked along the Seine as far as the Pont d'Alma, and then went down the steps leading to the riverside where the Yachting-Club de France had their moorings. In the golden light of the afternoon the calm stretch of water looked even more lovely, close packed with the white hulls and delicate rigging. Manou let Patapon out of his cage, but he had to bundle him back almost immediately, for there were dogs wandering along the riverside that threatened the plump brown and white rat with a sticky end. For two whole hours they inspected the pleasure squadron moored alongside the *quai* between the two bridges, hoping to see it suddenly raise sail and head for the sea which seemed so close. Even Daniel forgot the doubts and uncertainties that nagged at his heart.

At last, a little before seven, he decided to return to the hotel.

'I wonder if we'll find Mummy and Daddy have arrived?' Manou asked him as he took his hand.

Daniel hurried on without answering. He felt almost guilty at having allowed this short outing, until, as he passed the expressionless face of the hall-porter, he realized that there was still no news and that this would be another evening on their own.

'No, Monsieur and Madame Quint still haven't arrived,' the receptionist told him, 'and there have been no telephone messages for you.'

Dinner that evening was much less cheerful than the night before, despite the constant kindness of the head-waiter. Daniel merely played with his food, his main concern being to see that Manou did not disgrace himself, for he seemed wildly excited by the prospect of an extension of their bachelor life.

'Those two boys are so sweet,' a lady at a nearby table was saying. 'Perfectly charming!'

Daniel felt flattered, but a moment later his face clouded as he overheard a tactless waiter whisper behind him:

'No, the mashed potatoes are for the two orphans. Number 8.'

That was their table. The stupid remark abruptly brought him a clear understanding of their situation. Until now, all he had done was to wait patiently in accordance with Grandfather's 'movement orders', but the wasted day changed everything and had shifted the burden of responsibility. Inexplicably, there was still no sign of his parents and now it was up to Daniel, and Daniel alone, to take charge. Yes, he had to do something and after dinner he decided to discuss it all with the kindly Monsieur Hébert.

'Why get so upset about it?' the manager said soothingly. 'Your parents are a few hours late, that's all. There's no need to make a fuss. In any case, your grand-parents will be here tomorrow evening; I have their letter here on my desk.'

'True enough!' a frowning Daniel agreed. 'But the trains won't be running by then and I'd like to make sure that Grandfather has made arrangements to come up by road.'

'And how are you going to do that?'

'I'm going to telephone the Hotel Rosaria at Vittel,' Daniel announced firmly. 'Then my conscience will be clear. I should have done it as soon as I got back from the station this morning.'

'Is there any point?' asked Monsieur Hébert, somewhat annoyed.

Despite his irritation, he personally asked the hotel switchboard to make the call. Manou, meanwhile, had not let go of his elder brother's hand and seemed greatly impressed by all these comings and goings.

'Three hours' delay to Vittel,' the girl announced a few moments later.

Daniel looked at the clock in the foyer – it was barely eight-thirty.

'Your grandfather won't be very pleased if you wake him up in the middle of the night.' Monsieur Hébert laughed. 'Would you like me to get in touch with him?'

'No, I'd rather talk to him myself,' Daniel answered stubbornly. 'You don't know Grandfather!'

'Just as you like, then. I'll ask the switchboard to put the call through to your room.'

The two 'orphans' went upstairs, Daniel feeling better for having done something. He wished he had thought of it before. Manou responded well now that he had cheered up.

'Can I play with Patapon, or do I have to go straight to bed?' he inquired impishly, ready to take his opportunities as they came.

'You can play, but don't make too much row,' Daniel said with grown-up condescension.

He could see that the play would not last long, so first of all he gave his young brother a shower and put him into his pyjamas. Then he left him the bedroom in which to racket around with his beloved guinea-pig. In fact, by nine o'clock Room 617 was quiet and all Daniel had to do was pick Manou off the carpet and tuck him into bed.

'Kiss Patapon,' he murmured sleepily.

'Done it,' Daniel chuckled. 'Patapon was already dreaming five minutes ago. Now close your eyes and join him.'

A few seconds later Manou was sleeping soundly.

Daniel preferred not to get undressed. He had still not given up all hope of his parents arriving late that night, so he sat up on his bed with the telephone on the side-table within easy reach. Now his brain began to sort out his suppositions into a logical order. In the first place, Grandfather would get into a towering rage as soon as he knew that the children had been left to fend for themselves. However, his tantrums seldom lasted long, and in any case he had complete faith in Daniel. Secondly, since there had been no word from Mummy and Daddy, in all probability they had, somehow or other, got in touch with Monsieur Quint at the Hotel Rosaria. What would happen after that? Daniel had no idea where the two passengers from the *Armoric* might be, but, whatever the answer, Granny and Grandfather were sure to come hurrying to the Hotel Régina. Yet how were they to get to Paris? Monsieur Quint was quicker than anyone when it came to getting out of a jam, so Daniel was sure that he would either have booked seats on a coach or hired a car as soon as he learned that the railwaymen had come out on this wretchedly inconvenient strike. In other words, all would end in hugs and laughter.

'What a fool I am, making such a fuss about nothing,' Daniel said to himself and shut his eyes.

The subdued burr of the telephone woke him with a start. It was midnight by the clock in the room. He had been asleep for a couple of hours; his body was stiff and cramped, and his poor head muzzy.

'Your call to Vittel,' the girl on the switchboard said in a high-pitched voice. 'Be quick. Long-distance calls are restricted to three minutes. You're through now.'

Daniel recognized at once the strong Alsatian accent of Monsieur Muller, one of the proprietors of the Hotel Rosaria.

'Hullo, this is Monsieur Quint's grandson. . . . Yes, that's right, Daniel. I've simply got to talk to my grandfather! Please wake him up, it's really urgent!'

At first Monsieur Muller could only stutter into the telephone. He seemed confused.

'Your grandfather?' he said at last. 'He left suddenly last night with Madame Quint for the South of France. Didn't you know?'

'He can't have!' Daniel shouted in dismay. 'You must be making a mistake.'

'I'm certainly not!' Monsieur Muller bellowed. 'I drove them into Epinal myself and they just managed to catch the Strasbourg–Ventimiglia express.'

'But what happened?'

'Earlier in the evening Monsieur Quint had a telegram from the police at Saint-Raphaël to tell him that your uncle Jules and his family had been in a bad accident near Esterel. . . . Can you hear me all right?'

'Yes,' Daniel gasped. The room seemed to turn around him.

'Even if their train only got as far as Marseilles, your grandparents will be there by now. . . .'

'Where?' cried Daniel. 'I've got to get to them somehow!'

'I don't know, but Monsieur Quint left me this message, if your father should eventually phone through to Vittel; he wants all four of you to stay on in Paris and wait for him to send you news and instructions from the South of France. He'll do this as soon as ever he can. . . . Did you get all that?'

'Mummy and Daddy haven't arrived yet!' Daniel cried, in a shiver of panic. 'I'm all on my own here with Manou. . . . What are we going to do?'

'All you can do is wait, Daniel. Everything will straighten itself out in a few hours' time.'

Another voice cut in.

'Finish your conversation, please, caller. I shall have to cut you off now.'

Daniel began to scream like a lunatic and to babble frenziedly in an attempt to keep this ardently-desired link with the outside world which broke their isolation for a few brief minutes. Then there was a click and it was lost. He put down the receiver and wiped the sweat from his forehead.

In the darkest corner of the room Manou had woken up. He blinked as he looked across at Daniel.

'Why were you shouting like that?' he said crossly. 'You were naughty – you've woken Manou and Patapon up!'

'It's all right.' Daniel forced a smile. 'I had a nightmare. Go back to sleep.'

He got up to tuck Manou in, and kissed him on the forehead and Patapon on the nose.

'We're in a fine mess now.' He sighed as he, in his turn, slid between the sheets.

3

The Two Telegrams

GRANDFATHER'S telegram arrived the next morning at about eight o'clock, just as Daniel had finished dressing. Leaving Manou to stay in bed until breakfast came, he went down to the reception-desk at once.

Monsieur Hébert was there already. He himself handed the envelope to the boy whose face was so pitiably strained with anxiety. The message was addressed to *Monsieur Pascal Quint*, *Réginotel*, *Paris*. Daniel at once saw his grandfather's meticulous hand in this, for the old man always made a particular point of using telegraphic addresses.

'Open it,' said Monsieur Hébert, guessing why Daniel hesitated. 'You're quite within your rights as your father isn't here. I'd do the same if I were in your shoes.'

Daniel took out the fold of paper, fearing the worst, but he began to breathe again when he smoothed it out and read the message.

TURIN FAMILY INVOLVED IN CRASH ESTEREL – JULES ELVISA SLIGHTLY HURT – CHILDREN SAFE – DON'T WORRY – GO CHIBERTA DIRECT – DETAILED INSTRUCTIONS THERE – WILL JOIN YOU ROAD OR RAIL FOUR OR FIVE DAYS OUTSIDE – LOVE – FATHER.

Then Monsieur Hébert read it while Daniel briefly told him about his telephone call the night before. The manager grumbled when he noticed that the telegram had been sent off from Saint Raphaël at five o'clock the previous afternoon.

'Scandalous!' he said. 'Fifteen hours to transmit an

urgent message like this. . . . What are you going to do, young man?'

'I've only Mummy and Daddy to worry about now,' Daniel replied, his anxieties at last diminishing. 'A whole day has gone by already, and that's a long time to take to get from Le Havre to Paris. Before today is over, they're bound to let me know something. The main thing was to have better news from the South of France – and instructions from Grandfather. Now we've got them!'

He found things looking much simpler in the bright morning sunshine.

Two pairs of travellers were leaving the hotel, followed by a porter bent beneath the weight of their luggage.

'Are the trains running again?'

Monsieur Hébert shook his head despondently.

'It's still the same: the strike goes on, though there is a restricted service on some lines. But you have to be at the station to find out.'

'I'll stroll down there this morning,' Daniel decided, brimming with hope. 'In any case we can't just stay on at the hotel indefinitely. Manou's been as good as gold so far, but once he starts getting bored, life won't be so easy for me.'

He retrieved the telegram before turning to go.

'I'd rather have it by me. You never know.'

Monsieur Hébert put a gently restraining hand upon his shoulder.

'I know you're a sensible, trustworthy boy, but I'd rather you didn't hang about too long in the streets. I'm holding myself responsible for the pair of you until your parents arrive.'

Daniel promised not to linger more than was absolutely necessary. However, one idea had begun to take possession of his mind – it was up to him alone to make good the failures in Grandfather's elaborate plan.

Manou was only too happy to be going out, and he did not mind whether or not they took Patapon with them. When the two brothers returned to the Gare Saint-Lazare, they found it just as chaotic as it had been the day before. The station was packed with an angry crowd which seemed to be hoping against all reason for some miracle to take place. The ordinary police had been joined by special security squads, and this made the atmosphere all the more tense.

Daniel's hold on Manou was as good as a pair of handcuffs as they made their way through the press and reached the ticket-barriers.

The arrival board was completely bare and the tracks deserted. A very self-satisfied, well-dressed and talkative gentleman was saying his party-piece in front of a dozen poor wretches sitting dejectedly on their luggage.

'A strike's just like a bad cold!' he fluted. 'It can just as easily last six weeks as six days. And you can't do anything about it. It goes in its own sweet time.'

Not far away stood a policeman. He noticed the two boys standing alone, looking round as if they didn't know what to do. His interest aroused, he came over to them.

'Looking for someone, then?' he asked gruffly with a smile.

'We'd come to see if there were any trains,' Daniel answered evasively.

'Well, there aren't any, as you can see. These people are all wasting their time.'

The policeman had a kindly face that inspired confidence, but some instinct warned Daniel not to say too much. Furtively he squeezed Manou's hand in an attempt to put him on his guard, but it was too late.

'Then Mummy and Daddy won't be coming today?' the little boy cried, wide-eyed and afraid.

The policeman had been going away but now he turned back abruptly.

'Are you on your own in Paris?'

Daniel saw the catch in the question.

'Oh no!' he answered quickly. 'We're staying with relations in a hotel.'

Then he fled, dragging Manou firmly behind him. He was unimpressed by this show of anxiety for his welfare. He was quite capable of looking after himself, no matter how black things might be.

A young man in a crumpled sports coat was leaning against the ticket-barrier. He had noticed this brief encounter and observed the look of uncertainty on Daniel's face. As the policeman turned away, Manou came completely into his view, the boy's neatly-brushed fair hair having a golden, almost white, sheen in the blinding sunlight that poured through the glass roof of the station. The young man jumped away from the barrier to slip round behind the two boys, fumbling as he did so at the leather case slung round his shoulders.

Daniel was thinking only of getting away. Half-running, he dragged Manou towards the gloomy flight of steps leading to the kiosks below at street-level. They were halfway down when a voice rang out behind them.

'Hi, you kids!'

As they turned round there was a blinding flash. Daniel had just time to see a shadowy figure running up the top steps to vanish against the glare into the station.

'Whatever was that?' Manou asked, frightened.

'I don't know. Must have been some photographer . . . . Can't think what he was up to. Maybe he was just testing his flashlight . . . . Come on!'

The incident, coming on top of the policeman's questions, made Daniel uneasy. Had he been on his own, he wouldn't have taken a scrap of notice, like any other boy of his age, but it was different with Manou there. He would have to be very careful.

They went into the shopping arcade where the cheerful bustle of the crowd calmed Daniel slightly. As they walked past the mirrors in the window of an outfitter's shop, he glanced at their reflections to make sure there was nothing odd about their appearance. Of course Manou looked very smart in his light flannel suit, but that was not enough to cause a riot or to set police and photographers on them.

Daniel had another move in mind. It had occurred to him during the sleepless hours of the night before, and he was sure that Grandfather would approve of his acting so methodically. Scolding Manou, who wanted to stop in front of every shop window, he walked swiftly up the Rue Auber to the offices of the North America Line.

The commissionaire at the door directed him to the Passenger Information Service and he had the good luck to go to the right counter at the very start.

'Could you please tell me,' he carefully asked the clerk, 'whether Monsieur and Madame Quint did land at Le Havre yesterday morning from the *Armoric*. They are my parents, you see.'

'I can check that easily enough,' was the immediate reply.

The clerk, a kind, bald-headed little man, thumbed carefully through a sheaf of passenger-lists, removed the one for the *Armoric* and ran his pencil down it. Then abruptly he lifted his pencil in a gesture which betrayed his astonishment. Daniel hardly dared to breathe.

Slowly the clerk looked up.

'You're quite right, Monsieur and Madame Quint did cross on the *Armoric* and they *had* booked their passage to Le Havre. But the note I have here shows that they disembarked unexpectedly at Southampton, at about seven o'clock yesterday morning.'

At first Daniel could not believe it. Yet again Grandfather's plan had proved faulty. It was almost as though there was a conspiracy to isolate the boys completely. All the same, when he thought about it, although this bad news did nothing to settle their difficulties, it did at least have the advantage of showing them exactly where they stood.

He whispered his thanks.

'I don't suppose you've had any news from them?' the little clerk added sympathetically. 'A lot of people have been in the same situation since yesterday. This wretched strike has upset everything. But don't worry, your parents aren't far away. You'll just have to wait a little longer.'

Waiting, waiting all the time, that was all they could say, and all this worry, and little Manou to nurse like a new-laid egg, and never being able to relax for a single moment! None of this bothered the youngster, who now tugged impatiently at his older brother's hand.

'I know! I know!' Daniel muttered. 'You want Patapon and it's time for lunch. And it doesn't matter if I kill myself worrying in the meantime. . . . All right, then, let's go back to the hotel.'

The clerk called him back.

'Would you like to leave your address with me? You never know, it might come in useful. When things are as uncertain as they are now, it's always a good thing to let as many people as you can know where you are.'

Quite unsuspecting, Daniel willingly told him.

It was past twelve o'clock when he got back to the Hotel Régina. He was relieved to be there, for he felt safe. A group of Americans in the foyer surrounded Monsieur Hébert, talking loudly and laughing, and although Daniel would have liked to tell him what had happened, he realized that it was the wrong time to interrupt – the manager had plenty to keep him busy. Furthermore, the two young boys, who had not twenty years between them, were occupying a fine suite of three rooms!

A bell-boy intercepted them as they were going into the restaurant. He held out a telegram.

'This has just come. Is it for you?'

Daniel saw that it was addressed to *Monsieur César Quint*. That was Grandfather. What fresh trouble did it hold? This time he had no scruples about opening it and his heart lifted when he read the sender's name – *Pascal*. At last there was news from his father. The telegram came from London, where it had been handed in the evening before.

IMPOSSIBLE COME PARIS – LAST-MINUTE SUMMONS BOARD-MEETING TRANSBUILT-ALYSON – WILL JOIN YOU DIRECT CHIBERTA 15TH OR 16TH – FLYING LONDON–BIARRITZ – LOVE TO DANIEL AND MANOU – DEEPEST APOLOGIES – PASCAL QUINT.

That was that! Five short lines shattered completely the slender hope that still remained to Daniel. Although he had been half-expecting it, this final blow made him angry. 'Now it's Uncle Jérôme's turn!' he said bitterly to himself. 'The *Président Dupas* can't help losing her propellers in the first rough sea they run into. What a business! Well, after all this, I know someone who won't write another "movement order" in his life – not even to send Manou to the grocer's on the corner.'

During the meal Manou never opened his mouth except to put in food, and never raised his eyes from his plate. This eventually began to worry Daniel.

'What's the matter?' he asked. 'Something wrong?'

The little boy looked up and frowned at his brother.

'I'm very cross,' he muttered reproachfully. 'You get telegrams all day long. You open them, you read them and you never say a thing. It's not fair, I want to know too.'

Daniel could conceal the news no longer. He forced a cheery look on to his face as he tried to announce the disasters as if they were not so serious.

'Granny and Grandfather won't be coming to Paris,' he said off-handedly. 'They've had to go to the South of

France to help Uncle Jules. He's had a lot of trouble with his car.'

'What about Mummy and Daddy?'

'They've stopped for a little while in England. You know what it is, Daddy gets so busy with all his work that he can't always do just what he wants.'

Manou was not deceived for a moment. His face went red, his lips puckered – tears were not far away.

'Then we're all by ourselves!' There was a tremor in his voice. 'Whatever will happen to us? I want my Mummy. . .'

'Don't look like that, you old silly!' Daniel patted him on the cheek. 'We came all the way from Vittel by ourselves all right and we'll manage the trip to Chiberta just as well. Once we're down there, you'll see how all the rest of the family will turn up in a few days. Now you're not going to get yourself all scared of being with me, are you?'

'But the trains aren't running,' the little boy objected, suspiciously. 'So we'll have to walk all the way, like you said in the story.'

Daniel burst out laughing.

'Of course not! We'll go by coach. They run everywhere. That was all people could talk about at the station this morning. . . . You just wait. Why, it'll be the best trip you've ever had!'

Manou let himself be soothed, but Daniel realized that he was on the alert. The charm was broken, and from now on the little boy would take fright at the least provocation. All the same, this brief commotion had had one good result – it had strengthened Daniel's resolve to take the one reasonable way out of their predicament.

After lunch, he went straight off with Manou to see Monsieur Hébert in his office. The manager read Pascal Quint's telegram and did not hide his annoyance. Daniel seized the initiative.

‘We can’t hang about in Paris for ever,’ he said, with a shrug. ‘I think we should leave for Chiberta as soon as ever we can.’

‘But you might get fresh news very soon.’

‘I don’t think so. Both my grandfather and my father have their own problems, and neither knows what the other is doing at the moment. On my side, I haven’t a temporary address for either of them and we’ll risk wasting four or five days more if we try to get in touch to tell them what has happened. And even when we do, we shall only be told to hurry down to Chiberta – which is precisely what I plan to do now!’

‘Why Chiberta?’

‘First of all because I want to do what Grandfather told me. Then, in any case, the family has to meet there next week. Lastly, my brother and I will be at home there. The keys are with the caretakers of the villa next door, and they will look after us until the others turn up.’

On the tip of Daniel’s tongue was a fourth reason, which he did not dare to mention. Monsieur Hébert put it tactfully.

‘Don’t forget,’ he said, ‘that if you stay here too long, the hotel bill will be a heavy expense for your parents. But what really worries me is your travelling alone. Can’t you wait at least until the strike is over?’

‘Even if it ends today, it’ll be two or three days before the railways start working properly again,’ Daniel answered, determined to get his way. ‘We might just as well leave here and now. Manou is getting terribly bored and I shan’t be happy until I can let him loose in the garden of the Villa Etchola!’

‘All right then, you’ve decided to leave – but how will you travel?’

Daniel spoke of the coaches that had been brought into service on the main inter-city routes and Monsieur Hébert at once telephoned the Grand Palais. There an emergency centre had been established that morning to organize and coordinate road transport.

'Twelve coaches allocated for the Bayonne-Biarritz route,' the switchboard girl told him after a moment's pause, 'leaving at regular intervals between three and five o'clock this afternoon from the Esplanade des Invalides.'

'We'll go by one of those coaches,' Daniel cried.

Manou cheered up at once. The trip sounded a lot of fun to him.

Monsieur Hébert felt some qualms about letting the two boys set out, all on their own, on a long and tiring cross-country journey.

'They promise luxury coaches,' he warned, 'but you'll probably find they're just old lorries with a couple of broken-down benches in the back. Wait until this evening. A lot of guests have their cars with them and some of them are sure to be going towards Bayonne. They'd be only too happy to take you with them.'

'I'd rather go in a big lorry,' Manou said.

'You wait and see!' Daniel sighed. 'No, the best thing we can do is take our chance. It'll be just too bad if we reach Chiberta in the middle of the night.'

'What about your luggage?'

'I've only got an overnight bag, and all Manou has is Patapon's bird-cage. So we're not overloaded.'

Monsieur Hébert gave way. When all was said and done, he would be glad to have the three rooms.

The two boys were off to Number 617 in a flash. Daniel shoved his washing things and his spare clothes into the red and grey bag his grandmother had lent him, while Manou shut Patapon in his cage and gave him a meal of lettuce.

Despite the excitement of their departure, Daniel's heart

sank when he thought of money, for he knew he would be presented with no small bill for their stay.

They swept through the room like the wind, leaving on a table the roses they had bought for their mother. The flowers had not even begun to fade.

Downstairs, Monsieur Hébert was waiting for the boys. In his hand was the bill. Daniel shook in his shoes.

'Have you enough money to pay for your coach-tickets?' was the first thing the manager asked.

Then, when Daniel said he thought he had, he gave him some fatherly advice. Next came the bill. Monsieur Hébert had generously knocked off the 100 francs which the far-sighted Monsieur Quint had sent him when he had booked the rooms, so there was next to nothing outstanding, a mere 15 francs.

'Give the bill to your grandfather.' The manager laughed. 'I'll let you have credit.'

But Daniel had his pride and he made it a point of honour to pay this balance with the cash which he had left. They said goodbye to their friend the manager. Everyone had been so kind to them – waiters, bell-boys, liftman – everyone except the tall commissionaire in his admiral's uniform, who now watched them leave with the look of an ogre.

At the very moment when the two Quints left the Hotel Régina hand-in-hand, the little clerk in the North America Line offices, who had answered Daniel's enquiries a few hours before, opened a copy of an evening paper fresh from the press. His attention was at once caught by a photograph on the front page. He gave a low whistle. A few seconds later the bald-headed clerk lifted his telephone receiver and dialled the number of Interpol-Investigation, a detective agency regularly used by the legal department of the North America Line.

'Monsieur Barboton, please.'

His call was put through immediately.

'That you, Barboton? Seen the evening paper? . . . Which one?'

'*Europe-Soir.*'

'Good. See the picture on the front page?'

'Say that again! Had my eyes glued to it for the last ten minutes.'

The picture showed two frightened young boys halfway down a badly-lit flight of steps. It bore the caption:

Lost in the maze of a vast Parisian railway-station, these two boys may well be the young Jackson-Villars. The family lawyer, Monsieur Kern, has officially identified Benny (*left*) from this photograph. It is one of fifty taken by our team of reporters at the nerve-centres of the capital. The search continues . . .

'Oh, what fools these reporters are!' Barboton snorted. 'A lot of help, I must say! Where on earth are we to pick the kids up now?'

The little clerk cleared his throat as if to emphasize the importance of what he had to say.

'They were at the office this morning – at my counter! The elder one asked me for some harmless piece of information, which may have some bearing on the case, all the same.'

'That's fine, but how do we pick them up again?'

The bald-headed little man lowered his voice.

'We keep to the old arrangement?'

'Of course we do!' Barboton retorted crossly. 'You can count on your ten per cent. When I make a promise I keep it!'

'The elder boy used the name Quint – obviously made-up – and was silly enough to leave me an address,' the clerk went on. 'Of course it may be a false one, too, but you can check it easily enough.'

'Come on, tell me!'

'Hotel Régina, 124 Avenue Marceau.'

Then, as Barboton was making a quick note of it, he added,

'You going to pick them up right away?'

'You crazy?' The other chuckled. 'Read the rest of the article and you'll understand. I'm not the one to kill the goose that lays the golden eggs. If you really have got on to the Jackson-Villars kids, I'll simply keep my eye on them for the time being . . .'

'Well, don't hang around too long,' the little clerk said before he hung up. 'You aren't the only one after them, you know.'

4

The Cross-Eyed Man

THE page-boy swooped down from his post at the entrance of the Hotel Régina to open the door of the smart yellow taxi with the white roof that had just drawn up outside the awning.

'Monsieur has no luggage?' he asked, and then repeated his question in English.

The object of his inquiry shook his head and leaned forward to speak to the driver. Summing up the chances of a tip, the page-boy examined him closely from head to foot. Barboton, the inquiry agent, was dressed in a drab-coloured suit which hung on him like a sack, but did not hide his grubby shirt-collar and cuffs. On his head was a light green felt hat, stained and pulled down over his eyes. Convinced that this deplorable exterior did not conceal some millionaire, the page-boy stared the visitor brazenly in the face, only to look away in some embarrassment.

Monsieur Barboton was afflicted by the most appalling squint. Not that it was any disadvantage to him in his professional activities, for who would realize that he was under the detective's observation when he had no idea in which direction Barboton was looking?

The page-boy slammed the door shut and the driver moved some ten yards or so on to leave the hotel entrance clear. At that moment the hall-porter came out to take up his post under the awning and noticed the peculiar customer approaching, his right eye staring towards the Eiffel Tower and his left towards the Sacré-Coeur in Montmartre.

'Excuse me,' Barboton asked confidentially, 'but are some children called Quint staying here?'

The admiral-of-the-fleet had been trained not to give free information, and he now frowned and cocked his head like someone who is a trifle hard of hearing. The inquiry agent took the hint at once and slipped a note into his hand.

'The Quint children have just left the hotel.' The hall-porter winked as he made his announcement. 'Definitely! Took their luggage with them, too.'

Barboton mopped his brow in his agitation.

'Gone long?'

'Not much more than ten minutes ago.'

'Where were they off to?' the private detective asked anxiously and produced another note.

'As far as I know,' the hall-porter murmured, 'they were making for the Esplanade des Invalides, where they hoped to get on a coach for the South-west.'

'Anyone with them?'

'All on their own, just as they were on the day they arrived,' the hall-porter assured him with a knowing look. 'There's something fishy about those two, but if you'll take my tip, you'll watch out for the elder boy. He strikes me as having a mind of his own and he's not going to let anybody push him around.'

Barboton jumped into his taxi.

At either end of the Esplanade des Invalides portable crush-barriers had been set up and the enclosed space was like a fair-ground with its motley crowd that shifted in the wake of the enormous coaches creeping forward in low gear to their picking-up points. Each time one of them stopped it was at once stormed by shouting travellers, elbowing and shoving aboard to get the best seats.

Along the pavements a number of hastily-painted signs

showed the various destinations, the prices of the tickets and the approximate times of departure. Squads of police tried to bring some order to this chaos and to calm the near-riots caused by the announcements made over the loud-speakers attached to the lamp-posts. The July sun beat on the vast tarmac square. The few trees round it were already wilting and gave little shade.

Barboton strode round this temporary coach-station, shouldering aside the bystanders, his cross-eyes swivelling from left to right with extraordinary swiftness. When he reached the crush-barriers that marked off the place where the coaches left for the South-west, he nearly trampled two boys under foot. They were standing a little to one side in the shade of a chestnut-tree under whose branches a score of travellers sat in a huddle to enjoy the illusion of coolness. At the feet of the elder of the pair lay a red and grey check hold-all, and with head bent he was carefully counting and re-counting a slender wad of bank-notes. Under the younger boy's arm was a little bird-cage containing a reddish-brown and white creature. He watched what the older boy was doing with keen interest and his almost silver fair hair shone like a sunbeam in the deep shade of the tall chestnut-tree.

Barboton moved a few paces away and breathed a sigh of relief. From his pocket he carelessly produced a paper, glancing first at it and then at the fair-haired little boy. At that instant the latter looked up, to see the stranger watching him from a distance. Having checked and re-checked his money, Daniel bent down to pick up his bag and then tried to take Manou by the hand.

'What are you squinting for?' he suddenly asked.

The little devil shook his head, as though shaking off a fly. The two boys left the shade of the chestnut-tree to plunge into the furnace of the crowd. Twenty yards behind them came the cross-eyed man.

'Have we got enough money?' Manou asked, his own eyes back to normal.

'I think we'll be all right,' Daniel answered unconcernedly. 'Once we've bought the tickets, we should have enough for two or three meals – so long as you don't expect a feast! At the moment what we've got to do is get a couple of seats on one of these coaches, and that's not going to be easy . . .'

Next to two brand-new coaches, one green, the other blue, stood an enormous lorry. The tail-board was lowered and they could see the primitive seating arrangements inside.

'We'd be better off in the lorry,' Manou announced, sticking to his original idea. 'Lorries kick up more dust and go much, much faster.'

'We'll take a seat where we can get one!' Daniel was cross. 'Come on!'

Hundreds of people had picked up their luggage and were shouting and shoving against the double line of burly police which protected the vehicles. On the pavement three queues wound their slow way aboard between the crush-barriers. Daniel strove to make the few yards to these corridors, but the burden of Manou, who would not let go of his hand, and of the hold-all, which tried to trip him up, was too much and in the end he had to give up.

They took refuge under the chestnut-tree once more to get their breaths back. The blue coach with every seat now taken was already drawing slowly away to the angry shouts of the discontented left in its wake. A white and gold luxury coach took its place.

'Let's have another try.' Daniel sighed and picked up his bag.

'Where are you kids going?' a friendly voice behind them asked.

In the shade of the tree stood a plumpish man. There

was a wicked twinkle in his eye, but his red face wore a kindly smile. Over his shoulder was slung a leather satchel, on his head was a conductor's cap with a black peak and round his left arm a blue and red band to which was pinned a badge with the coat of arms of Paris. Daniel's spirits rose.

'We want to go to Bayonne.' He laughed. ' But by the look of things we'd do better to start walking.'

'Don't give me that!' The man guffawed. 'It's too easy! I'll see you safely through with a wave of my hand. All you've got to do is get into the middle queue – it's for the passengers with priority. I'll let you have your tickets right away and you'll be off on the next coach as sure as fate. . . . All right?'

Daniel could not have hoped for more. The man twitched his satchel round to the front, with great ceremony took a counterfoil book out of it and tore off two numbered tickets.

'Let's see, now, two singles from Paris to Bayonne! The youngster'll have to pay the full fare like a grown-up, I'm afraid, there's no half-price on the coaches!'

He scrawled something mysterious on the tickets and handed them to Daniel, who gave him 60 francs in return.

'Well that's settled that!' said the conductor, snapping his satchel shut. 'Now just come with me.'

By making great play with his cap and coloured armband and by taking very little notice of other people's protests, he got the two boys into the second queue.

'There you are!' he called as he turned to leave them. 'Have a good trip!'

The people in the queue did not seem very pleased at having the two boys thrust so irregularly among them.

'But we've paid our fares already!' Daniel pleaded, waving the tickets in their faces.

These, however, did little to soften the discontent and

the young queue-jumpers were only forgiven because of Manou's charm and the peculiar object he carried in his bird-cage. Packed to the doors, the gold and white coach pulled off in its turn and was soon replaced by a large and comfortless lorry.

'You've got what you wanted now,' Daniel said to Manou. 'But we'll be choked with dust by the time we reach Chiberta.'

The queue moved slowly forward. The boys followed the stream and by cunning use of their elbows gained another dozen places. Now it was their turn. Only two seats were left, right at the back of the lorry. Daniel had their precious tickets ready and let go of Manou's hand to give them to the driver. The latter was for a moment reduced to silence.

'Somebody's played a trick on you,' he said at last, while everyone around them laughed. 'These tickets aren't worth the paper they're printed on. Now you pay for your seats or push off.'

Daniel crimsoned as he protested.

'I've just paid sixty francs for those two tickets! Look, the man wrote our destination on them.'

'What man?'

'A fat chap, with a cap and a satchel.'

'You've been robbed, sonny!' The driver shrugged. 'There's nothing I can do about it.'

A policeman had come up. He looked at the tickets and questioned the children suspiciously. A few kindly travellers had gathered round as Daniel took his brother by the hand once more, desperate at the situation into which they had fallen. His grandparents were at the other end of France, his parents were in England, Chiberta was nearly five hundred miles away and he had not a penny in his pocket.

But of course there was still one way out of the wood – the thick manila envelope Grandfather had entrusted to Daniel to pass on to Pascal Quint. There should be some money in it, and, in view of their position, there could be nothing wrong in opening it now. Daniel prised open the flap with his finger and glanced furtively at the contents – month-old letters, a few business papers, a sheet of squared paper folded in four (what a joke – it must have been Daddy's 'movement orders') and . . . a cheque. With an angry gesture Daniel stuffed the envelope back into his pocket. He felt on the verge of panic. Manou pressed tight against him, his head lowered, weeping silent tears that splashed on to the pavement. Seeing him so upset restored some of Daniel's courage. He was responsible for Manou and it was up to him to carry on through thick and thin; above all he had to protect his younger brother from the hundred and one mean little tricks that make life hard and ugly.

The policeman summed up the situation.

'No parents, eh, no home and no money? No point in your hanging round here. Let's go and see the superintendent. He'll tell you what to do.'

From then on Daniel thought only of escape. One step deeper into this mess and it was all up for Manou and him.

Police headquarters lay within four wireless trucks parked in a hollow square in the middle of the Esplanade. There, wearing his silver-braided kepi, sat a sour-faced superintendent. He listened impatiently to the policeman's report and immediately sent some of his men in search of the bogus bus-conductor. Then all he did was to glare at the prey that had been brought in to him while he continued a bitter monologue to the two gentlemen with him, each with worried face and rosette of the Legion of Honour in his buttonhole.

'The strike has paralyzed the holiday rush and as a result I've never seen anything like it. For the last couple of days Paris has been so full of lost children that we don't know what to do with them all. The Prefect was saying something about lodging them in one of the University hostels, but he's a bit late in the day. You'd need all the army camps in the area, and still you wouldn't have enough room!'

Of course he was exaggerating, but Daniel shivered when he realized that their fate was in the hands of this sour-tempered, sharp-tongued man.

'What do you want me to do with these two?' the policeman asked in a scared voice. 'They haven't the money to carry on.'

'Right!' the superintendent barked at Daniel. 'Tell me what happened.'

Daniel took it calmly, and explained as clearly as possible the plans for a family reunion made by Monsieur Quint and how a series of mischances had caused their complete breakdown.

'What the devil's all this rigmarole?' the superintendent thundered when the tale was over. 'Take these two brats away,' his fists waved above his head, 'and keep an eye on them. I'll deal with them later!'

'And make sure you take their surnames, Christian names and descriptions!' one of the other gentlemen added fiercely.

Daniel and Manou hung their heads as they emerged from the shelter of the wireless-trucks. With their police escort they felt like prisoners. A temporary Reception Centre had been set up nearby in a shady square. It comprised a First Aid Post, a free canteen which supplied only cold water, and a few Red Cross helpers who did not know which way to turn. Into this cluster of exhausted folk anxiously waiting for news, for the unlikely advent of practical help, or simply for an end to the chaos which had disrupted their harmless existences, the policeman gently but firmly pushed his captives.

'Stay there and don't try to run away!' he told them. 'It'll do you no good . . . and it won't do me any either.'

The two boys sat down side by side on a wooden seat and gradually recovered their spirits. In Daniel's mind had been the ghastly fear of having Manou torn away from him. He could imagine him all on his own, cut off from the warmth and love of his family which until now had always been his and which from now on Daniel alone must provide. The superintendent's angry outburst caught up with him at last in the terrified realization of the damage one man's overzealous or unthinking action could cause.

Manou had got over his fright and was chattering away to Patapon quite normally.

'Of course we could always lie low in the Régina,' Daniel spoke seriously to him. 'Monsieur Hébert would always look after us. But the way things have been going, we'd be stuck there for a week or ten days at least. . . . So you've just got to show what you're made of because if we're going away now, and going to reach Chiberta, it's not going to be a picnic.'

'I'll show what I'm made of,' Manou promised confidently. 'What have we got to do?'

'Get out of here first! After that we'll see.'

Their policeman, a young man with the look of a countryman about him, was walking up and down outside the entrance to the Reception Centre with two colleagues. Every now and then he would stop, swing swiftly round and cast a worried glance towards the two boys, at the same time raising a threatening forefinger, as much as to say, 'You just stay put, eh?'

A few minutes passed like this. Daniel looked all round him to see the lie of the land. The space allocated to the Reception Centre in the gardens of the Esplanade des Invalides was marked off simply by an ordinary rope run from tree to tree.

'Don't drop Patapon's cage,' Daniel whispered to Manou, 'and when I tell you, jump off the seat. I'll pick up my bag and we'll both make a break for it. But don't run whatever you do, or all the silly fools will start shouting "Stop thief!"'

'Okay!' Manou was thrilled at the idea of this game of hide-and-seek.

'And if anyone stops us, we'll say you wanted to be excused.'

Suddenly two travellers came over to sit on the boys' seat. The boys politely edged up to make room for them. The man was a skinny red-headed fellow and it was an obvious relief for him to put down the two enormous suitcases with which he struggled. His freckled face was open and pleasant. His wife was quite young. She smiled at Manou and poked her finger between the bars of the cage to stroke Patapon's soft fur. They soon struck up a passing friendship, under the influence of which Daniel told them all his troubles.

'We've been in the same boat as you all day.' The red-haired man sighed. 'But a moment or two ago someone gave me a tip which may mean that we can finish our trip without having to spend another penny.'

'What do you mean?' Daniel asked eagerly.

'Well,' their new friend went on, 'it seems that long-distance lorry-drivers coming up from the country have a sort of headquarters near the Halles – the Place Beaubourg. At any time of the day or night there are always lorries setting out for places all over the country. These drivers are decent fellows and they're always ready to take a passenger or two . . . and sometimes they don't want a thing in return. When my wife and I have got our breath back we're off to find this Place Beaubourg. With a bit of luck we may even be in Aubenas by tomorrow morning. . . . My, this has been a trip!'

They cooled off and then, with an encouraging word to the two prisoners, staggered away with their cases. The policeman was still there, but his movement on his beat had drawn him appreciably to the left, towards the coaches, and he turned less often to glance at the boys. Gently Daniel groped for his bag, leaned towards Manou and then stopped short.

'So you've got it again?' he growled. 'How long do you think you're going on squinting?'

Manou shook with laughter.

'I can't help it,' he said. 'Every time that man looks at me, I have to copy him.'

'Which man?' asked Daniel, suddenly anxious.

'That big man in a green hat, over there. The one trying to hide behind that tree. Didn't you spot him? He's as cross-eyed as a crab!'

Daniel took a furtive look at their watcher. The latter pretended to have his eyes elsewhere, which was not very difficult with a squint as bad as his. However, everything about him suggested that he was a professional sleuth, hot on an interesting trail.

'A little while ago,' Manou added, 'he was watching us when we were under the chestnut-tree.'

Daniel gritted his teeth. Not only did they have the police round their necks, they now had to escape what were probably the awkward attentions of the over-inquisitive. At once each and every casual passer-by seemed suspicious.

Luckily the man disappeared into the crowd. For some minutes there had been sounds of a disturbance from the nearest picking-up point, from which the coaches left for the Riviera. Suddenly the boys saw police reinforcements hurrying along the Esplanade des Invalides. Their own policeman and his two colleagues were staring towards the place from which the noise was coming and they must have seen some signal, for almost at once they strode towards it without looking back.

'Let's go!' exclaimed Daniel, and picked up his bag.

A little later the creators of the disturbance, three excitable gentlemen from Marseilles, were arrested and conveyed under strong guard to the mobile police-station. As the ill-tempered superintendent was giving them a piece of his mind he suddenly noticed that in their escort was the young policeman who had brought Daniel and Manou to him.

'Where are those two kids I told you to keep an eye on?' he barked.

'In the Reception Centre. They've been very good and haven't even moved.'

'With no one watching them?' The superintendent's voice rose to a scream as he grew still more savage. 'Bring them here at the double! Two to one those little liars are the Jackson-Villars children . . .'

5
Place Beaubourg

AT five o'clock that evening Daniel and Manou were still wandering along beside the Seine, between the Pont-Neuf and the Pont Notre-Dame, trying to find an invisible Place Beaubourg.

Although it was cooler by the river in the shade of the great plane-trees, their leaves shimmering in the breeze, tiredness had begun to slow the fugitives down. Every five minutes Daniel stopped to swap the two burdens that sapped his strength – the red and grey check hold-all which had seemed so light when they set out and was so heavy after two hours' wandering, and Manou, whom he had now almost to drag along, his little legs being quite unable to keep up with the long strides of his elder brother.

'The Place Beaubourg? Never heard of it!' was the answer given by everyone whom Daniel asked.

Needless to say, this did not include policemen. Whenever Daniel met one, he began to whistle as though he hadn't a care in the world and he hurried past looking the other way.

At last a fat woman who was selling newspapers outside the Hôtel de Ville was kind enough to explain the mystery.

'No! No! There's no such place as the Place Beaubourg.' She laughed. 'That's what the lorry-drivers call an empty lot where they park their trucks. It's over on the other side of the square at the end of one of those streets on the left.'

Five minutes later Manou and Daniel rounded a corner

in the old Rue Quincampois and emerged into the sunlight of a vast empty space bounded by grimy houses, scaffolding and mounds of empty crates. Lorries were parked in apparent disorder on the rutted ground, on which could still be traced the twisting line of the old streets and the foundations of the old houses. The lorries

were of all shapes, makes and sizes – old ones and new ones, with sparkling or dingy paintwork – and around them bustled men in greasy overalls, their sleeves rolled up to the elbows.

'It was kind of that man.' Daniel's face beamed. 'He wasn't lying. Keep going just a bit longer, Manou, and then we can have a rest. You'll get your ride in a lorry. Come on!'

Manou had perked up already and was looking about him curiously. All that remained was to find a kind-hearted driver who would give the two castaways a free ride. This, however, might not be easy in this queer encampment, and Daniel made up his mind to go round asking at every lorry, trailing after him his wretched bag, Manou and Patapon.

The good luck which had favoured their escape was waiting for them here in the Place Beaubourg. Daniel had only gone a short way when he spotted, peering through the side-window of a dusty lorry, the friendly face of the red-headed man. His wife was sitting beside him. The driver was not yet aboard, but the engine was gently ticking over.

Gaily the two passengers hailed the boys.

'Didn't take us long, eh?' the man called to Daniel. 'We'll be off in a minute or two, and then . . . tomorrow morning we'll be having breakfast in Aubenas!'

He guessed at the regret and envy in Daniel's shy smile.

'Don't you wear yourself out chancing your luck in this ant-heap,' he added slyly. 'Shall I tell you why? Most of the drivers you can see are looking for another load, so they don't even know where they're going or when they're setting off. So what do you have to do? It's easy. You just go straight to that little blue café on the corner of the Rue Saint-Martin, Charlot's. A haulage agent has his office in the back room. He gets a call for a lorry to take such and such a load to such and such a place. He calls it out and whichever driver wants to go that way takes that load.'

'What do I have to do?' Daniel asked.

'Go to the lady at the cash-desk, Madame Julie. She's very nice and she'll have a word with the agent for you. As soon as there's a chance – and you won't have to wait long – she'll let you know and away you go!'

At once Daniel could see that his troubles might be at an end. The driver came running, a sheaf of papers in his hand, swung himself up into the cab alongside his two passengers and the heavy lorry moved off. As it swished past the two boys, the red-headed man and his wife waved happily to them out of the window.

'Let's have a look at Charlot's,' Daniel said as he picked up his bag once more. 'It'll give us the chance of something to eat.'

The little blue-fronted café did not seem up to much, but it bubbled with activity and re-echoed within to booming voices. A dozen privet-bushes in their pots protected the outdoor tables which were shaded by the fully-lowered awning.

Daniel dropped his bag and made Manou sit down.

'I'm going to see the lady,' he told him. 'Just you sit still and don't get off your chair.'

'Can I let Patapon out?'

'Yes, but don't let him run round on the ground. It's no time for a game of hide-and-seek!'

Shyly he went inside the café. The front room was dim and cool. Along one side of it was a bar at which some fifty brawny characters were talking and joking at the tops of their voices as they swigged their beer and guzzled enormous sandwiches. The telephone was ringing all the time and as it shrilled above the hubbub of the customers, they would put down their glasses or stop chewing and all turn their heads in the direction of the back room.

'Ten tons of jam for Marseilles and Nice!' shouted a raucous voice. 'Pick up in the southern suburbs. Eight centimes the kilo! Any takers?'

Two or three men elbowed their way through the crush, others came hurriedly in from outside to find out what was offered and to signal to friends delayed at their lorries. People shot in and out, shouts went from one line of parked lorries to the other, and soon there was the deafening thunder of a lorry starting up nearby. A huge truck eased out, swaying between the lines of parked lorries, to vanish with a roar down a neighbouring street.

The lady at the cash-desk looked as nice as the red-headed man had said she was. However, she frowned slightly when Daniel told her his troubles and his urgent need to be on his way. She leaned forward to look at Manou through the front window of the café.

'As a general rule, drivers won't take kids unless there's a grown-up with them,' she told Daniel. 'It's too easy to find yourself in trouble. . . . How do I know you haven't run away from home?'

Daniel bit his lips. The sudden question made him understand what sort of suspicion can fall on a child alone in a large town or trailing along the roads with little or no luggage. The chaos caused by the strike would only make this state of vagrancy seem all the worse to the outsider observing it with a lack of sympathy or full understanding. Busybodies and policemen seldom have time to look below the surface: in their eyes any child abroad without money or resources may be a budding delinquent on the run.

'If you want some proof, here it is!' said Daniel, producing the two telegrams from his pocket.

He explained the awkward situation created by his grandfather's and his father's each relying on the other and thus, quite unwittingly, abandoning the boys to the tender mercies of the first idiot who came along. It could all be blamed on the bad luck which had struck the beautiful schemes drawn up by Grandfather. The lady behind the counter did not stop serving beer or buttering bread as she listened enthralled to this strange story.

'Each of these two telegrams,' Daniel finished, very reasonably, 'ends with the same instructions – meet me at Chiberta! So you see there's really nothing else to be done and that's why I want to be off to Bayonne just as soon as I can.'

'I'll have a word with Monsieur Charlot,' said the lady,

nodding towards the back room. 'But I can't promise anything, mind. You'll have a very long wait. . . . Half the night, perhaps. . . . Go back to your brother outside and don't go away. Would you like anything to eat?'

Daniel stammered his thanks.

'I should like something for Manou,' he said at last. 'A cup of chocolate and some croissants, please. I've still a little money left. Enough to last until we get to Chiberta.'

Everything seemed to be going like clockwork. At their table outside, Manou was laughing and chattering away to a dozen burly lorry-drivers, who looked as though they might have been made of solid oak. Daniel was not worried, for he felt safe among these perpetual travellers whose only thought here was to enjoy a few minutes' relaxation before picking up a profitable load for the homeward trip.

His younger brother had brought Patapon out of his cage and was showing him off like a performing-dog. The little creature was not in the least alarmed, but begged for a few crumbs, jumped over the huge hands held out to him, scuttled up on to a shoulder and ran down again into his cage when he was told to. His squeaks and gambols delighted his audience.

'I'll buy him off you!' one of the men proposed to Manou. 'He'll be company for me in my cab. How much do you want?'

'A million!' Manou hazarded to test the enthusiasm of his fans.

There was a howl of laughter, and then the shrill of the telephone scattered the audience.

'Fifteen tons of plate-glass for Strasbourg!' bellowed Monsieur Charlot from the depths of his den. 'Express rates, ten centimes the kilo! Any offers?'

The high rate hushed their voices, but after a few

seconds the conversation swelled again. It was all a friendly and straightforward matter of arrangement.

'Well, Louis, I could do it if you could take my ten-ton load to Nancy. You'd lose two centimes the kilo on it, but we could settle that up later on.'

'All right!'

A white-haired old waiter brought Manou's chocolate and croissants and set a lime-soda, which he had not ordered, in front of Daniel.

'Plenty of time,' he said, when Daniel offered to pay. 'Your train hasn't been signalled yet.'

'You heard that?' Daniel turned to his young brother. 'Don't hog your food. Make it last; we're going to be here for quite a while.'

Towards seven o'clock, as the shadows of the neighbouring houses were lengthening, a group of policemen appeared at the end of the short Rue Pierre-au-Lard. They came closer, looking about them, swinging their whistles, and started to wander up and down, glancing in the driving cabs, questioning the odd driver, peering under a badly fastened tarpaulin, running their eyes over the Place Beaubourg with a show of unconcern which deceived nobody. It was not usual to see them there, as Daniel realized from the sudden change in the atmosphere of the café. Some of the customers came to the door where they stood silently watching what was going on.

The outside tables were more or less hidden from the street by the screen of privet-bushes, but Daniel's heart pounded as one of the policemen came towards the little blue café.

'Sit still,' he said, gripping Manou's hand. 'If I stand up, make yourself as small as you can, get behind me and slip inside the café.'

Although there was nothing to suggest that they were the people the police were after, he was on his guard all the same. Manou and he had left the Reception Centre with remarkable speed and the police do not like people to take their leave of them so abruptly.

The policeman walked away to the right as though ignoring the outside of the café, then, turning suddenly, passed close along the privet-screen without seeing the boys. His companions were waiting for him at the end of the Place Beaubourg. They talked together for a moment, staring round perplexedly, and then made off at the same saunter the way they had come, up the short Rue Pierre-au-Lard.

It took Daniel a minute or two to get his breath back. A driver came over from parking his lorry. He carried a thermos flask in his hand and an empty haversack was carelessly slung from his shoulder.

'The police are looking for a couple of kids,' he said in a loud voice as he came into the café. 'There's been something about them in the papers it seems.'

His news fell like a stone into a smooth pond. Daniel dared not look round. He could feel people staring at him through the café window. The telephone in the back room never seemed to stop ringing.

'Emile! I've got your load for you,' Monsieur Charlot called. 'Nicely coupled up. Six tons for Limoges, six for Bordeaux and six for Bayonne. I got you five, eight and ten centimes the kilo. That all right by you?'

'I'll say!' Emile shouted, pleased.

'Bayonne! Our train's coming in,' Daniel muttered to himself. 'We'd better not miss it.'

'I want to play outside with Patapon,' Manou said and got down from his chair.

'This is a fine time for playing,' Daniel complained. 'Sit still and stop monkeying around. Everyone's watching us. If we miss this lorry it'll all be your fault!'

There was the tap of a finger-nail on the window behind

them, and Daniel turned, wild with hope. The lady signalled to him discreetly, but the look on her face was discouraging. He slipped into the café and went up to the counter.

'Monsieur Emile would have been glad to take you with him,' she whispered in Daniel's ear. 'But the police-search looks bad. And that's not all of it, you just take a look at this . . .'

She handed him a newspaper, and Daniel felt his hair bristle as he opened it carefully and saw the photograph from the *Europe-Soir*. There was the stairway in the Gare Saint-Lazare; and while you could only just recognize him, Manou's pink cheeks and fair hair were plain as a pikestaff. He jumped when he read the caption.

'Read the article, too,' the lady whispered.

The whole business was neatly summarized in a dozen lines. Steve and Benny Jackson-Villars belonged to a wealthy Franco-American family. They were spending their summer holidays in France on a paternal great-uncle's estate near Chantilly. Three days ago they had run away with little more than the clothes they stood up in, leaving a note to say that they were doing so of their own free will and that they had a perfectly good reason. The police had been informed at once. Madame Jackson-Villars was due to fly in to Orly that very evening, a day behind the family lawyer. Her husband was catching a plane from the Far East, where he had been on a business trip. While there had been plenty of conjecture about their motives, the only reasonable explanation for their running away, was that it was just a whim of two pampered rich boys, although a friend of the family had hinted that it might have something to do with the plans the parents were making for a separation.

'We've been caught in the silliest case of mistaken identity,' Daniel exclaimed indignantly. 'We're nothing to do with the Jackson-Villars. . . . The photograph . . . all right, it is a snap of the two of us. Someone took it this morning in the middle of the Gare Saint-Lazare. But I can't understand what Manou's face and mine are doing in it.'

'All the same, that's what's started all the trouble,' Madame Julie said softly. 'I'm quite ready to believe you, but it'll be a much longer job, and a harder one too, to convince the police, who are looking for what they think are a pair of runaways, and the newspapermen, whose main concern is a news headline. It'll be even harder to get my customers to take pity on you. They're decent people and they have a tough life, and if they have a spot of bother on the road or they get held up for some reason or another, it can cost them anything up to a couple of thousand francs. . . . So why don't you go back to your hotel? You were very happy there weren't you?'

Daniel shrugged.

'That would be jumping out of the frying-pan into the fire. Something tells me we'll be safer on the run than in a hotel where police and reporters can come and go as they please.'

'Go to a police-station and tell them just what has happened. Our local one is very understanding and it's only a few minutes away.'

'I'm not that stupid!' Daniel sneered. 'If we went in we'd never get out again. If I was on my own it would be a different matter. It'd be rather fun to pull their legs. But I've got Manou with me! I'm not having him passed from one department to another like a file of letters, having to answer all sorts of silly questions and being shouted at by a lot of oafs. But what I'm really frightened of – and it's worried me sick for the last three days – is getting separated from Manou and having to leave him suddenly all on his own, quite defenceless and at anybody's mercy. If anything like that happened my parents would be quite right to be really angry with me. I'm the oldest and I'm big enough to look after Manou. I don't care what we're up against, sooner or later I'm going to get him to Chiberta where he'll be safe and sound.'

'So you still want to go on?'

Daniel clenched his teeth and nodded.

'I'm so sorry for you!' she said. 'But I've got to play fair with my customers. I can't let them risk being held up for eight or nine hours, when they're carrying a load, for a business like this. If another run for Bayonne comes up, Monsieur Charlot will mention you to the driver. He'll also tell him that they're looking for you, rightly or wrongly, and . . . well, you'll probably still be here tomorrow morning.'

'How do you know? Maybe there'll be one of them who doesn't care about the police,' Daniel said with a feeble grin.

'For both your sakes I hope there is. But that's not all, by a long chalk. That photo in the papers can do you an awful lot of damage. By this time thousands of people will have seen it. So you be careful. Don't push your luck too far!'

Dusk drew in after eight o'clock and this made the strange Place Beaubourg even busier. The little blue café was always full. Monsieur Charlot's raucous bellow turned the place into a battle headquarters. Drivers leapt into their cabs, revved their engines and swung away down the made-up road running down the middle of the parking lot. Minutes later other heavy lorries would emerge from the neighbouring streets to take their place. Fresh faces, tanned by the sun, would cluster round the bar where Madame Julie, the lorry-drivers' and the lost children's fairy-godmother was busy.

Remembering the state of his purse, Daniel left supper to the last moment, and as he looked round to order their frugal meal he watched Manou out of the corner of his eye. But there was no need. Without being asked, the white-haired waiter brought them two large plates of mutton stew, a big chunk of freshly-baked bread, biscuits, fruit and a large bottle of lemonade.

'It's better than the Régina,' Manou kept saying, busy with his knife and fork.

Daniel, somewhat abashed, tried to pay, but every time he did so, all the waiter would say was,

'There's plenty of time, your train is still off the rails.'

Patapon the Great was let out on parole and sat at the head of the table watching the two eaters and waiting for his lettuce leaves or celery shoots.

Night fell at last, turning the poorly-lit square into a mass of shifting shadows through which the glare of headlights would suddenly cut a dazzling track. Daniel became more despairing as, one after the other, three lorries left for Bayonne. Madame Julie looked commiseratingly through the window. They would have to go on waiting.

On the stroke of ten a grey-haired driver came in, worn out with heat and fatigue. He dropped into a chair at one of the outside tables next to the boys. He ordered a beer and sank half of it at one gulp; then he turned to look at his neighbours. Patapon caught his fancy, and he smiled at Manou, who was half asleep, and winked and pulled a face at Daniel.

They exchanged a word or two.

'I'm waiting for a load.' The elderly driver sighed. 'It's always the same game. I'm getting on a bit now and my lorry is an old crock. She's not too fast and she can't manage the loads, so I have to make do with the left-overs, the loads at rock-bottom rates that nobody else wants – fertilizers, scrap-iron, bricks or cement. A wretched two or three centimes the kilo! Anyway, where do you kids want to go?'

'Bayonne,' Daniel answered. 'Or anyway as far as we can in that direction.'

'All right! Whatever happens, I'll be going to Bordeaux,' the driver explained. 'I'll take you three parts of the way, and when we get to Bordeaux, I'll find one of my mates to take you the rest of the way to the Basque coast for sure.'

In his enthusiasm, Daniel almost took the offer on the spot, but he felt in honour bound to warn his carrier.

'They're none too keen to have anything to do with us because of what's happened,' he said and took Madame Julie's paper from his pocket. 'The silly thing is that it's really nothing to do with us. . . . Here, read this.'

As the driver caught the import of the article, his bushy eyebrows gathered into a frown. Then he stared at the two boys, comparing them with the boys in the photograph. Daniel waited, without much hope, while he made up his mind.

'What's all this nonsense?' the driver grunted at last, with a roughness that was not unfriendly. 'Is your name Jackson-Villars, or isn't it?'

'No, it isn't!' Daniel protested. 'Our name's Quint. Our family comes from Bordeaux.'

'Ah, I used to know a Monsieur Quint in the old days. He ran a big export business with warehouses on the Quai Bacalan. . . . I started off as a driver with his firm.'

'He's my grandfather!' Daniel's voice rose and he could hardly speak for relief. 'And we're off to see him, at Chiberta, near Bayonne, and that's what all the trouble's about.'

He gave a clear explanation of what had happened and produced, in support of his story, all the documents in his hands, including his 'movement orders'.

'Ah, that's the old man right enough!' The driver chortled. 'If I'd only to pick up a couple of sacks of sugar from the other side of the town, old Monsieur Quint would scribble half a dozen pages of instructions for me. . . . Don't you worry, I'll take you, and the police can chase my old Berliet if they like.'

There was a commotion inside the café. Monsieur Charlot's voice could scarcely be heard above the din created by his customers. From knot to knot of drivers the message was shouted until it reached the tables outside.

'Ten tons for Bordeaux – any offers? Ten tons of heavy machinery, ten tons at top rates! No offers? . . . Peyrol? . . . Where's Peyrol?'

'Here I am!' yelled the elderly driver.

And he made for the back room, shouldering his way past the cheerful drinkers at the bar.

'Whew!' Daniel squeezed Manou's neck. 'This time I think we're there. Wake up!'

Madame Julie smiled knowingly at him through the window, and a moment later she left what she was doing to give the boys her parting advice in the gloom outside the café.

'I shouldn't attract attention when you go,' she said as she stroked Manou's fair hair. 'Sneak straight off to old Peyrol's lorry and wait for him there. I'll tell him what you've done. His is the old Berliet with the tarpaulin, parked behind those two red Fords. Hurry now!'

Daniel thanked her and again tried to pay his bill.

'Keep your money.' She laughed. 'You aren't home yet!'

She kissed a very sleepy Manou good-bye and the two brothers made off with their bag and their bird-cage, tripping over the deeply rutted ground. The Fords seemed to crush the Berliet with their size and smartness, but the darkness was deceptive. When they reached her, the old lorry was still imposing and her cab looked most comfortable.

Five minutes later old Peyrol came after them.

'You kids there?' he called gaily. 'We're off right away. I've got to collect my load from the Thomasson Works. It's on our route. You've brought me luck: five machine tools at ten centimes the kilo! They're packed for export so it won't be an awkward load. Why, you'll think you're riding in a Rolls!'

He opened the passenger door. Daniel heaved his brother on to the foot-rest, settled him on the broad seat inside, put Patapon on his knees and climbed in after him, arranging the bag along his thigh as a pillow for Manou.

'All right in there?' said Monsieur Peyrol as he swung himself aboard through the other door. 'Grand! It looks a fine night, but if the little one feels cold you'll find a blanket in the compartment above your head. Take the thermos and the sandwiches. We'll be glad of them first thing tomorrow morning.'

He switched on the headlights and started the engine. Its roar woke the echoes of the Place Beaubourg. Slowly the Berliet drew out on to the roadway between the lines of parked lorries. Monsieur Peyrol handled the machine with expert skill.

Daniel leaned out of the window, sniffing the breeze that fanned the sleeping city. He hummed to himself, drunk with the feeling that he was free once more, enjoying every second of their departure which put an end to two agonizing days.

Manou's head was already heavy on his thigh and he leaned still farther out, staring into the blackness that was all the more intense at the end of the empty streets. Monsieur Peyrol turned another corner and as he did so blinked his headlights in warning.

A prowler stood at the cross-roads. Suddenly the orange light swept over him and Daniel shivered as he saw that it was the cross-eyed man. There was the spy from the Esplanade des Invalides in his crumpled suit and his green hat, the dazzle of the headlights making him squint more horribly than ever.

6

The Crash

TWENTY minutes later the Berliet was easing through the gates of the Thomasson works at Bagneux. The lorry was expected, for they had hardly stopped before a night-watchman jumped on to the running-board to guide Monsieur Peyrol through the maze of yards and alleyways to the dispatch-shed. Simultaneously a string of arc-lamps snapped on, flooding their route with a cold white light.

With the ease of long practice, the driver backed his truck against the loading-platform. Storemen were busy with five tall, long, narrow, slatted packing-cases lined up below the gantry.

'Best thing for you to do, is stay in the cab and keep out of sight,' Monsieur Peyrol told Daniel. 'Won't take ten minutes to get her loaded up.'

Manou was still asleep, sprawling with his head on the hold-all. Not even the vibration of the winch, the dull thud as the cases dropped on to the back of the lorry or the screech of the steel cables tightening round the load – nothing could wake him up. Very gently Daniel took Patapon's cage from him and stowed it away under his right elbow. A little later he heard the tail-board slammed fast, the cheerful farewells, and then Monsieur Peyrol swung himself into the cab, happy to have his carrier's contract and the delivery-note for the load.

'I've got to get this lot to the Chargeurs Réunis by ten o'clock tomorrow morning.' There was a note of anxiety in his voice. 'It's running it a bit fine, but old Theophilus'

– here he gave the steering-wheel an affectionate pat – 'old Theophilus has done it before. I've filled up the tank, so all we've got to do is just drive straight on.'

As they left the works Daniel strained his eyes to scan his surroundings, but there was no one about. Now that Theophilus was under way and they were on board there seemed little risk, but the furtive appearance of the cross-eyed man at the very moment when they were pulling out of the Place Beaubourg, made only too good sense of Madame Julie's warning.

The last houses of Antony were behind them and the lorry was now tightly wrapped in the summer night. The road stretched ahead in the light of the headlamps as far as the eye could see, a straight and narrow border to the sleeping country-side, pulsating with life as holiday traffic and heavy lorries sped by in both directions. As they approached, they blinked their headlights, and as they passed, a wave of air buffeted the warmth of the cab. Theophilus roared steadily on, his ten-ton load holding him to the road.

'I never push the engine for the first few miles,' Monsieur Peyrol told Daniel. 'Once we're through Etampes, Theophilus will really get into his stride – a steady fifty miles an hour. Try and get some sleep, son, like the little one.'

'I'd rather see where we're going,' Daniel answered. He had never felt more wide awake.

'Okay! We can have a bit of a chat until we get to Tours, it'll help me to keep awake. . . . Light a fag for me, will you, you'll find a packet in front of you in the right-hand compartment.'

The old lorry-driver was now off on a flow of reminiscence about his wandering life.

'I've been all over France – north, south, east and west – and this is the best road of the lot, even in winter. Don't you worry, I know it like the back of my hand. . . . Accidents? You'll have one in the end. You can be as careful as you like, you may never take a single risk, always stop when you begin to feel tired, but one of these days your number will be waiting for you round some corner and you'll wake up in a field in the middle of a fifteen-ton load. If you own your own bus and it's in pieces, that little spot of bother's going to cost you forty or fifty thousand francs and you're back where you started from.'

His voice sounded cross.

'What really gets you down when you're on a long haul at night is to have someone sticking to your tail like the so-and-so that's been following me ever since we left Bagneux! His headlights have been blinding me in the mirror for the last twenty minutes. If I accelerate, he puts his foot down too, and every time I slow up he does the same. I'm going to pull in to the next lay-by and stop a minute. He'll jolly well have to pass me then!'

Daniel stuck his head out of his window to try to see, but the back of the lorry loomed like a wall beyond the side of the cab and blocked his view. Monsieur Peyrol slowed up, pulled into the side of the road and gently brought Theophilus's fifteen tons to a halt.

The beams of the headlights of the car behind them grew brighter as it approached, and then a smart yellow taxi with a white roof slowed as it passed the lorry and disappeared at last in the distance and darkness of the road.

'If he doesn't go any faster than that, I'll have him under my feet again in another five minutes!' Monsieur Peyrol grumbled. 'Ah well, off we go, Theophilus!'

As he started the lorry, he launched once more into what was now a one-sided conversation, for Daniel hardly uttered another word. His eyes were glued to the road and only left it occasionally to glance at his wrist-watch. They were through Etampes and Theophilus began to speed along the wide, straight roads through the Beauce. The speedometer needle began to flicker around the fifty mark. They reached Orleans at about half-past one in the morning.

'We're running to schedule.' The driver sounded pleased. 'If Theophilus can make us an extra quarter of an hour, we'll be able to stretch our legs when the sun comes up beyond Châtellerault.'

They had just left the town when, to his horror, Daniel saw a line of about a dozen red rear-lights stationary in front of them. Two policemen were ordering all the heavy lorries to pull in to the side of the road. Only the holiday traffic was allowed to pass in low gear the narrow bottleneck of the road-block. Monsieur Peyrol guessed what was worrying the boy.

'Don't get so upset.' He laughed. 'They're only Traffic Inspectors checking the delivery notes and the load. The rest's no business of theirs.'

Their turn came and Daniel hugged Manou, crouching down on the seat to make himself as small as possible. Monsieur Peyrol stopped the lorry, opened the door and climbed heavily down. Two men examined his papers by the light of their torches and then all three walked round the lorry. The tail-board came down with a clatter and, feeling Manou stir, Daniel looked round. His young brother's eyes had opened and he was slowly waking up.

'Have we stopped?' he asked, rather puzzled.

'Don't worry,' Daniel whispered. 'We'll be off again in a minute. Lie still and keep quiet, or else Monsieur Peyrol may get into trouble because of us. . . . You never know.'

The three men came striding round to the front of the lorry. As Monsieur Peyrol pulled the door open, one of the torch-beams happened to be pointing inside the cab. It dazzled the two boys, who closed their eyes.

'What's all this?' said one of the inspectors. 'Carrying passengers?'

'Like everyone else now the rail strike's on,' replied Monsieur Peyrol. He stood with one foot on the foot-rest. 'Anyway, they're only my nephews.'

'Got any proof?' the other inspector asked with a nasty snigger.

Monsieur Peyrol got down deliberately.

'I don't need to give you any proof,' he said drily. 'My cab's my home and if I like to carry my whole family round with me, it's none of your business, now is it?'

His bluntness so disconcerted the questioner that he did not press the matter any further. The engine roared into life and Theophilus accelerated down the empty road, through the cloudless night with the scent of new-mown hay around them. The moon had risen and by its light they could see on their left glimpses of a broad pathway of white sand and a line of shimmering water. It was the bed of an almost dried-up River Loire.

Manou had gone back to sleep again with his head buried in the hold-all. The brush with the inspectors had somewhat lowered Monsieur Peyrol's spirits and he did not speak again until they were through Blois at about three in the morning. By then Theophilus had made up the lost time, and the driver allowed himself the luxury of a word or two.

'I've still got someone on my tail,' he said angrily, when Daniel had lit a cigarette for him. 'Can't tell if it's the same one, but I can't get rid of the brute, that's for sure. Well, we'll try another trick. Watch this, son. I know a good spot round here. I use it sometimes to sleep in.'

He put his foot down and the needle of the speedometer flickered up to fifty-five and steadied there. In the distance the posts marking a bend were white in the headlights. Monsieur Peyrol swung Theophilus into it almost without reducing speed. They had just passed Amboise and bend followed bend with so little interval between them that Theophilus swayed from left to right and right to left with a pleasant rolling motion. As they came out of the last bend, the driver jammed on the brakes, swung the wheel hard over and the lorry vanished abruptly under an archway of tall trees down a track sloping gently to the Loire.

'Here we are!' Monsieur Peyrol announced as he brought Theophilus round in a large grassy clearing.

He stopped the engine, switched off the headlights, leaned out of the window and listened. The track stretched in front of them like a tunnel at the end of which was the main road, bright in the moonlight. Daniel heard the hum of the car that was trailing them grow louder and louder. Its headlights flashed through the trees, and then it swept past without slackening speed.

'It's the same fellow all right,' Monsieur Peyrol murmured with a nervous giggle. 'That yellow taxi with a white roof! If he's got a passenger, there'll be a splendid lot on the clock! But I expect the driver's having a bit of fun. He'll think we're a good way ahead, and as the road's all bends from here to Tours, he'll shove his foot through the floorboards trying to get on Theophilus's tail. So we'll get shot of the crazy fool .... What do you say, son?'

Daniel forced himself to smile. He was enjoying his adventure, but his old anxieties had returned in force. He felt the butterflies in his stomach. 'Monsieur Peyrol doesn't want to frighten me,' he thought. 'All the same he can't quite make up his mind whether this wretched taxi is following us for fun or whether it really is shadowing us, as he thinks it may be.'

They each drank a cup of coffee. Manou moaned in his sleep, but did not wake.

'I'll get the blanket and tuck him up,' Daniel whispered. 'It's getting chilly, and it's so easy to catch cold.'

As skilfully as his mother, the boy managed to wrap Manou up without waking him.

'You are fond of your little brother, aren't you?' said Monsieur Peyrol.

'He's so small,' Daniel sighed. 'And it would make me so unhappy if anything happened to him.'

'Well, I'm not worried, he'll be all right!' The lorry-driver was full of confidence as he pulled the self-starter.

They were through Tours by four o'clock and already the eastern horizon was golden with the promise of another broiling day. As the light grew stronger, so the traffic thickened. Every minute Monsieur Peyrol would give a blast on his horn and a wave through his window as they met an old acquaintance heading for Paris at the wheel of his heavy lorry.

'It's a funny thing, you know,' he was telling Daniel, 'but you meet someone at the same time and the same place so often that in the end you get to know everybody. I've been giving a wave to some fellows as we pass for years now, and I've only said a couple of words to them in my life.'

Then they were through Châtellerault, and now Daniel began to feel so tired that it was an effort to keep his eyes open. The monotonous throb of the engine, the gentle sway of Theophilus, the warmth and quiet of the cab, all combined to send him to sleep before he was aware of it. He heard Monsieur Peyrol cursing some careless driver and then he knew no more.

It was the fact that the lorry had stopped that woke him up with a jerk. It was broad daylight and, already high in the sky, the sun blazed down on green fields, little valleys, woods and hedges. Monsieur Peyrol had switched off the engine, opened his door and was in parley with a hefty fellow standing on the grass-verge. It was another lorry-driver, with a sun-tanned face and curly black hair. His lorry was parked a little way away, its nose pointing towards Paris. Their clipped conversation echoed so clearly in the stillness that Daniel was at once alert, his heart beating wildly.

'They've put up the road-block right out in the country just over a mile ahead,' the black-haired driver was saying jerkily. 'It's not the usual check-up. They're stopping everyone including the tourists. The police are there in full force, with two squads of motor-cycle boys and plain-clothes inspectors. They want to see all your papers, even your insurance card, and they give you a proper going-over.'

Monsieur Peyrol flicked the dead butt of his cigarette on to the road. He was thinking.

'I don't want to tell you what to do,' the other man went on, 'but if you want to get through without any bother, I'd get rid of your passengers!'

In his embarrassment, the old lorry-driver turned his eyes, red-rimmed by fatigue, towards the boys.

'They're only kids,' he said at last. 'I can't just leave them by the roadside. Would you do it, Simon?'

Simon shook his head.

'Try to get round it through La Rochefoucauld,' he suggested. 'The road turns off about a hundred yards farther on to the left. It's narrow and it's bumpy, but that doesn't matter if your load's on properly. From La Rochefoucauld you make for Angoulême, and you'll be on the main road again. It'll put another half-hour on your schedule.'

Daniel was torn between the fear of being dropped off in strange country with Manou and their luggage, and that of getting their new friend into trouble.

'We'll get out, Monsieur Peyrol,' he said and shook

Manou's shoulder. 'It's the most sensible thing to do. If for some reason or other they were to hold us, it would muck up your trip.'

'You keep your nose out of this,' the driver growled back at him. 'You'd be better off getting hold of that haversack and giving your brother something to eat. That's it then: we'll go through La Rochefoucauld. . . . Thanks, mate!'

He slammed his door shut and started the engine. Theophilus moved sedately to the next intersection and then turned down a pleasant side-road which wound through the country. Suddenly the cab was full of the scent of the fields. Manou munched a sandwich.

'I did sleep well!' he said with his mouth full. 'This is the best ride I've ever had.'

His obvious enjoyment made Monsieur Peyrol smile and did something to dispel Daniel's growing disquiet. It was like being in the turret of a tank up there in the cab. They looked down on fields and woods. The road was clear ahead with here and there a tree growing at the side. Theophilus was so broad in the beam that now and again he would pull down an armful of greenery.

They met with no obstruction and by seven o'clock the little expedition was safely through La Rochefoucauld, where few of the inhabitants were up and about. It was there that Monsieur Peyrol must have taken the wrong turning. Daniel had hardly time to see the sign-post but the road seemed far narrower, its surface much more rough and he himself a million miles from Chiberta. They had their first near-squeak just over a mile farther on. Without warning a farm tractor shot out of a field towing a trailer. Theophilus squealed in protest as the brakes were slammed on and disaster averted by a hair's breadth.

'My fault,' Monsieur Peyrol growled as he recovered

from the shock. 'These little cart-tracks aren't built for old buses like mine.'

The needle of the speedometer dropped to twenty-five and stayed there. A little farther on the bushy slopes began gradually to rise on their right and the road dropped. Theophilus cut the first corners close, his offside wheels tearing at the bank. The horn wailed mournfully to clear the road. There was a long straight stretch and then once more a sharp corner. Almost without their noticing it, the needle of the speedometer had crept up to thirty-five. Monsieur Peyrol swung the wheel over to the right but the whole weight of the lorry seemed to bear to the left.

It was then that Daniel felt the ten-ton load press against his spine. This was what was making the heavy lorry speed blindly down the hill, for its brakes no longer held. He glanced at Monsieur Peyrol. The driver had gone white as he battled with his gear-change. A sinister snapping sound shook the chassis.

Ahead there was still a short straight stretch and beyond it a grassy field through which a stream flowed. The road, meanwhile, made one last bend before it crossed the stream by a narrow stone bridge and then gently climbed the slope on the far side. The needle of the speedometer was hovering around the forty mark. In a flash Daniel saw the crash coming and imagined the lorry smashing through the parapet, falling down the other side with a hideous din. As he saw it, he thought, 'We can get through, we've got to get through!' and his arm tightened round the shoulders of Manou who was innocently watching the road go by.

'Hold tight!' Monsieur Peyrol shouted, hurling himself to one side to get out of the way of the steering-wheel.

The bonnet smashed through the parapet in a shower of stones. Through the windscreen, Daniel watched the field coming up to meet them like a huge wave. There was a terrifying crash as the lorry hit the ground and bounced them all against the roof of the cab. Then, very slowly, it heeled over on to one side with a screech of rending metal . . .

Daniel was only out for a moment. He was surprised by the silence that immediately followed the accident. Where he was, huddled against the door, he could feel on his cheek something cool and sweet-smelling. It was the long grass of the field. An exhausted hiss came from the engine. Daniel looked up, and there through the other door was the blue sky. His own was the floor of the cab for the time being. On it lay the driver and his two passengers in a tangled heap of twisted limbs.

Monsieur Peyrol succeeded in freeing himself first, by pulling himself up on the steering-wheel. Manou was rolled in a ball against his brother, crying feebly.

'Any bones broken?' Daniel whispered anxiously.

There was no reply. Monsieur Peyrol managed to

straighten himself and to squeeze, with considerable effort, through the driver's window and out of the cab. His face was drawn. Daniel was now able to get to his feet and with great care he lifted his young brother out.

A few seconds later all three were standing safe and sound beside the carcase of Theophilus. Manou still sobbed. He had not the slightest trace of a bruise: it was delayed shock. All Daniel had suffered was a slight scratch in the middle of his forehead, caused by a splinter of glass. Monsieur Peyrol seemed unharmed, too, as he strode round his lorry wringing his hands. Theophilus was in a sorry state, his massive chassis snapped in two, his axles broken, his bonnet squashed flat and his mighty tyres blown out.

The force of the crash had been enough to toss half the load overboard. Two huge crates had fallen right into the middle of the stream. They lay there, half buried in the mud, forming a dam against which the water was slowly rising. Children from a nearby farm were already running down the slope towards them. They stopped at the roadside, staring stupidly at the crash.

'It's all our fault.' Daniel hung his head. 'You should have left us on the main road and gone on alone.'

Monsieur Peyrol told him off sharply.

'Don't talk such nonsense! The damage is done and I'm too old to make a fuss about it. . . . The main thing is that the three of us have survived without a scratch.'

At one end of the bridge was a mile-post that read – *Pranzac* 1½ *m*; *Angoulême* 10 *m*. Daniel wanted to make himself useful.

'I'll run to the nearest village and get help.'

'No point in doing that,' the old lorry-driver exclaimed. 'In five minutes' time we'll have the whole neighbourhood running up with the local policeman at their head. If they find you here it'll make things awkward. Take your brother's hand and make off as though you were just going for a walk, while you've still got time. We can't be much more than sixty miles from Bordeaux and you're bound to pick up a through coach in Angoulême. . . . Off you go now and stop arguing! That's an order!'

Daniel had to obey. Manou had somewhat recovered from the crash and was now looking round in bewilderment.

'Patapon?' he whispered sadly. 'Where's Patapon?'

Daniel climbed back into the overturned lorry. The cage had not shifted from where he had wedged it. Patapon was scrabbling against the bars with heart-breaking squeaks. Daniel handed the little creature out to Monsieur Peyrol, and after it the red and grey hold-all, the haversack, the blanket, the driver's small suit-case and the plastic folder with his papers in it.

'Cut across the fields and get on to the road higher up,' Monsieur Peyrol advised him. 'While you're doing that, I'll have a word with these local lads. . . . Come on, kids! Forget this business! One of these days you'll see me pull up at the front door of the Villa Etchola in a brand-new lorry.'

Daniel was not so sure, but he forced a grin. Monsieur Peyrol was in business on his own, the lorry was his, and he had lost everything in this sad accident. The load was covered by insurance, but he would only recover a fraction of what he would need to replace his old Berliet.

The lorry-driver shook Daniel's hand and ruffled Manou's fair curls. They were both about to go when he called them back.

'Here! Keep this!' he called to Daniel and threw him the haversack with the sandwiches in it. 'And take the blanket, too!'

7

The Bone-Shaker

A FEW minutes later the two wanderers were on the road to Pranzac. Daniel was carrying the red and grey bag and the blanket which he had rolled and strapped up, while over his left shoulder was slung the haversack. In the new-found isolation of the woods and the fields they were fairly safe and, for the first time, Daniel had allowed Manou to let go of his hand. Manou had only Patapon to carry and he was already looking longingly at the haversack – Theophilus's last leap had not taken away his appetite.

'Wait a minute!' Daniel said. 'When we've passed the first village. We were seen leaving the lorry, I'm sure of that, and the best thing we can do first is to get as far away as we can.'

Before setting out along the road, Daniel took one last look at the green hollow of the little valley in which the luckless Theophilus lay upon his side, like some dying elephant. By now the children from the farm were down in the field and staring at Monsieur Peyrol from a respectful distance. They listened while his deep voice and heart-broken gestures told them what had happened. Right above their heads was the broken parapet of the bridge and the slope sweeping down to the fatal bend that gaped into the empty air.

Daniel screwed up his eyes against the dazzling sunlight. A car with a glittering roof came into sight at the top of the hill on the far side of the valley and came slowly down the slope. It bumped across the loose stones on the bridge, stopped a moment by the milestone and then came along the Pranzac road. Daniel caught Manou by the arm and quickly pushed him into the bushes. The branches fell back behind them and there they crouched and hid.

The yellow taxi with the white roof was slowing down as it passed them and it stopped a hundred yards up the road. Stealthily Daniel put his head out from the leaves and looked round. The cross-eyed man was sitting in the front seat beside the driver, scanning the sunlit countryside. He got out, stretched his cramped limbs and looked up and down the pretty little road.

'This is as far as I'm going,' he told the driver in his harsh voice. 'If that confounded lorry hadn't overturned just at the right moment, we'd have lost all trace of it. Anyway, the boys can't be far away. I'd rather continue on foot. The taxi would put them on the alert.'

'Please yourself!' said the driver. There was a metallic click as he switched off his meter. 'You've had quite a ride, haven't you? With my return fare, you owe me 526 francs. I won't bother about the odd coppers. If we call it five hundred, I'll be quite happy.'

'I'll get it back and more, don't you worry!' The cross-eyed man chuckled as he produced his wallet.

While he paid up, Daniel wisely withdrew into the bushes. His initial fears had vanished in a few seconds, for he began to see that the snooper who was so discreetly shadowing them was perhaps less dangerous than the police in the large towns, or their over-inquisitive colleagues stationed along the main roads.

The yellow taxi made a U-turn, crossed the bridge once more and vanished over the brow of the hill. Daniel waited, listening intently. The man stood at the roadside, painstakingly surveying the lie of the land. At last his footsteps rang out on the tarmac as he set out swiftly towards Pranzac. Daniel gave him a ten-minute start, and this allowed them to finish a second sandwich. Then he eased his shoulders to the load and took Manou's hand.

'Get those little legs of yours in running order,' he urged. 'The rest of the way to Chiberta is going to be one long game of hide-and-seek.'

The only people they saw on the road were two old ladies dressed in black, a goat-herd, and a farm-labourer on a great cart-horse. They exchanged polite good-mornings. A police car whistled past them, bound for the bridge, so fast that Daniel had no time even to fear for his freedom. He walked along the grass verge on the right of the road, eyes firmly fixed on the way ahead and only occasionally glancing over his shoulder. There was no sign of the snooper; he must be well in front.

The road followed the line of a stream shadowed by willows, ran between a high garden-wall and a saw-mill and suddenly came out into the middle of the village, where the church overlooked the little square. It was barely eight by the clock. Very few people were about – housewives and shopkeepers at their doors, children with nothing to do already, and, under the signpost at the corner of the square, a dozen good ladies in their Sunday best, apparently waiting for something. They hardly noticed the two boys. Daniel saw at once the sign-post pointing to Angoulême and the rusty notice of the bus-stop. He made for the group with a determined air, for above all they must not linger anywhere, wander about as though they had lost their way or show the slightest hesitation – this was the one certain way of attracting suspicious attention to themselves.

'Don't get up to any mischief with Patapon,' he whispered to Manou. 'Don't let go of my hand and don't ask questions. If anyone speaks to you, let me do the talking.'

He turned to the ladies.

'What time's the bus, please?' he asked politely. 'We were afraid we'd missed it.'

'It ought to have been here ten minutes ago,' an old lady answered, laughing. 'Any other day, you *would* have missed it, my lad!'

The others looked kindly at the two boys, but did not speak to them. Manou was as good as gold. He had dimly realized that their wanderings were no longer an ordinary outing. Daniel let go of his hand for a moment while he secretly counted his money. He still had a five-franc note and a handful of small change, but how long would that wretchedly small sum last him?

On the other side of the square, opposite the bus-stop, was the village café. It was painted bright red and there were white curtains in the windows. The door was open to the morning air and through it could be seen a group of customers at one end of the bar. Daniel looked away at once. There was no point in worrying any more. If the cross-eyed man was there, the best thing he could do was to pretend he had not seen him.

There was a sudden stir among the good ladies around them. The bus from Montbron was coming in, raising a long wake of white dust. It was an antiquated piece of mechanical transport, its rattling coachwork coming apart at the joints, groaning under a mound of packages piled on the roof-rack – wicker baskets, chicken coops, sacks of corn, petrol cans and farm implements. A duck poked its neck out of one parcel.

The bus itself was very crowded. Nobody got out at the stop, but all the travellers from Pranzac, including the customers from the café, squeezed in somehow. Daniel and Manou were carried on the crest of the wave and left stranded between the seats, squashed by two enormous men who held a booming conversation, punctuated by bellows of laughter, over their heads. The fare to Angoulême was one franc a head but there were no half-fares for children. Daniel paid up, furious to think of his sixty francs which had gone for good on the Esplanade des Invalides, and all to no purpose.

Otherwise there was not much to complain about. Less than an hour after the accident, the boys had joined the full flood of holiday-makers heading south. The Montbron bus stopped at a square in Angoulême which was a picking-up point for long-distance coaches, and its passengers fell out on to the broiling pavement. The boys waited their turn to get out, laughing at all the hurly-burly. Daniel could not see out of the back of his head, but some second sense told him that somewhere in the crowd someone was watching them. Hanging around behind them in the press of people was the passenger from the yellow taxi, his frightening persistence disguised by his absent-minded manner. To begin with, Daniel took no notice of him. Manou needed a hot drink and Daniel took him to a table outside a café and made him drink a cup of chocolate. Daniel himself went without; he had to make his money last. The waiter was a pleasant-faced young man who was quite ready to spend a few minutes advising the travellers in distress.

'Don't waste your time here,' he told Daniel. 'The coach operators have struck a little gold-mine at the moment, and they won't take a farthing off their fares. Best thing you can do is to go out of town where the road turns off for Châteauneuf. The cars have to slow up there and sooner or later you'll find someone who'll give the pair of you a lift.'

Daniel pulled a face. He had just emerged safely from one awkward situation which might well have landed him in trouble, and he was not going to be foolish enough to walk straight into another. On the far side of the square lime-trees made a shady corner screened by the old town walls. He took Manou over, sat him on an empty bench, and left him in charge of the luggage, telling him not to move away.

'Shan't be long,' he said and pointed to the square. 'I just want to have a word with those coach-drivers. I don't like having to beg for someone to take us the rest of the way. If the fares aren't too high, we'll get the next coach to Bordeaux.'

It was not long before he knew better. He could not have bought even a half-ticket for Manou with the money he had left. It was enough to make him lose hope altogether.

'Go to the Town Hall,' someone told him. 'For the last day or so they've been running a special service for all the people who've either broken down or run out of money. They won't say no, if you ask them for a little cash.'

Of course that was out of the question. A small crowd had gathered round the door of the coach to hear the boy telling his story to the driver. With measured tread a policeman approached from the other side of the square. Daniel saw him just in time. He beat an angry retreat, cursing the stupid curiosity of those who had nothing better to do than draw him to the attention of the police.

Manou was still there on the bench, but behind him was a stranger who had come out from behind a tree-trunk. To his horror Daniel saw that it was the cross-eyed man in his crumpled suit, his deplorable green hat pulled down over a face made still more ugly by a two-day growth of beard. His nervous laugh as he leaned over Manou did nothing to improve his expression and he was trying to snatch away the bird-cage which the little boy clutched desperately between his arms.

Throwing prudence aside, Daniel lowered his head and charged in like a young bull. The anxiety he had endured in the last few days gave him strength, and seizing the cross-eyed man by both shoulders he pulled him violently over backwards. The man lost his balance and came down with all his weight on his backside, his green hat rolling six feet away.

'What are you doing to that little boy?' Daniel's voice was angry as he prepared to go into the attack once more.

The cross-eyed man picked himself up off the ground, rubbed the dust from his hands and stepped a few paces back, taken off his stride by the suddenness of the attack.

'Have you gone off your head?' he stuttered in embarrassment. 'I wasn't even touching the kid. I only wanted a closer look at his pet.'

'You keep away from us!' Daniel growled from between his teeth. 'If I find you hanging around again, I promise you'll be sorry for it!'

Manou still sat there, terrified.

'Oh, so I can't go for a walk if I want to.' The cross-eyed man sniggered. 'This is a public garden . . .'

'You've been following us ever since we left Paris,' Daniel spat back, and clenched his fists. 'Why?'

'You're imagining things, sonny.' The man shrugged. 'We've just happened to meet in the same places, that's all. If you don't like it, why don't you call a policeman?'

That was the last thing Daniel could do, so he pretended not to have heard.

'I don't know what you're after,' he whispered threateningly. 'But something tells me you're following the wrong people. You'll go a long way before you get back the five hundred francs your taxi cost you.'

This reference seemed to surprise the cross-eyed man, but did not upset him.

'I'm not so sure of that as you are,' he said with treacherous mildness. 'Why don't we both go and tell our story to the police? They could soon settle the argument between us, couldn't they?'

Daniel had nothing to say to that. Some people sitting on the next bench got up and came over somewhat hesitantly, drawn by the sounds of argument. Keeping one eye on the snooper, Daniel backed towards the seat, carefully collected his luggage and gripped the hand that Manou stretched out to him.

'Come on, Manou,' he whispered. 'Don't be frightened, I'm here to take care of you. That bully can't hurt us.'

They took the first road down from the upper town. Daniel's dignity would not allow him a backward glance, but Manou looked over his shoulder several times.

'That man's gone away,' he said at last, very pleased with himself.

'I only wish you were right!' Daniel sighed. 'But I don't care whether he follows us or not. We'll get to Chiberta all the same, and he won't be so keen to look at Patapon there, I can tell you that!'

Reassured, Manou laughed. It was only a little after nine; the cool of the morning still lingered in the shady streets, and there was not a cloud in the blue sky – everything round them told them to forget their troubles. They hurried on.

Two and a half miles out of town Daniel found the spot the waiter had told him about. The almost endless flow of south-bound traffic had to slow down slightly when it came to the road forking off to Châteauneuf and Cognac. At a glance the boy could see that all the hitch-hikers had made for the same place. Campers, local people, young soldiers, all those who normally went by rail or hadn't the price of a coach ticket were standing waiting for someone to take pity on them. Competition was hot. As soon as a kind-hearted motorist pulled up, it was one mad scramble for the lifts he offered.

Daniel made three unsuccessful attempts and then gave up. If they were to walk to the next village Manou would have to have a rest, for he was beginning to lag behind. They both sat down on the verge, in the shade of the tall plane-trees planted alongside the main road. There were only two sandwiches left in Monsieur Peyrol's haversack and that was hardly enough. At noon Daniel set out in quest of something to supplement this and came back with some fresh bread, some cold meat wrapped up in a piece of paper, a pound of cherries and two small bottles of lemonade.

It was a cheerful picnic. Comfortably ensconced in a ditch, the two boys tucked into their food, enjoying to the full the continuous performance at the fork on the road. Daniel was spitting out the last cherry-stone when a cyclist collapsed with a great clatter on the grass verge in front of them. With an airy kick at his machine, he flopped down and lay for several seconds with his arms stretched out, puffing like a grampus. He was a bright young spark of seventeen or eighteen in khaki shirt and shorts, wearing on his head a stocking cap with a bobble at the end. It made him look like a clown and he hooted with laughter when he saw the look of astonishment on the boys' faces.

'I take my hat off to those slaves on the Tour de France!' he lisped. 'I left the Cité Universitaire the day before yesterday and all I've done is just over three hundred miles – barely a couple of medium stages – and here I am, believe you me, whacked, winded and good as done for. If I stood up the first puff of wind would blow me away, and that's the honest truth!'

'Like a drop of this?' Daniel asked politely and passed him his half-empty bottle of lemonade. 'It's still fairly cool.'

The student emptied the bottle at one gulp and licked his lips. Then he stared at the two boys.

'What are you kids doing here?'

'We're waiting for a car to give us a lift,' Daniel replied. 'It's a fight to get a seat, but we're hoping there won't be so many people in a few hours' time.'

The student sat up painfully and looked around him with lively interest.

'I give up,' he said suddenly, and unstrapped the huge mountaineer's pack fastened to the luggage rack. 'I think I'd snap in two like a twig if I tried to drive the pedals of this machine round once more. I'm going to take my chance at the turn-off.'

'You'll find it a lot easier to get a lift if you're on your own,' Daniel said, to encourage him. 'But what'll you do with your bike?'

'Would you like it? It's a write-off as far as I'm concerned. I can tell you after three hundred miles or more, my behind's been rubbed red raw!'

'I've got no money,' Daniel sighed. 'Or at least, hardly any.'

'Well, you can have it for nothing,' the student exclaimed. 'A scrap merchant wouldn't give me a couple of francs for that lump of old iron. If you do thirty miles on the old Bone-Shaker, you can knock me over with a feather.'

He limped off without hearing the heartfelt thanks which Daniel stammered after him. However, his clownish appearance must have helped him considerably in the struggle at the turning, for five minutes later he swept past, his face beaming as he sat singing at the top of his voice in the upholstered luxury of an enormous American car. Daniel hardly dared to believe their luck.

'The bike's ours now!' he said as he stood up. 'I don't know if I'll get very far, it's so hot, but I can have a try all the same. What do you think, Manou?'

'I don't mind – *I* shan't be pushing the pedals!' his young brother replied.

Daniel took hold of the old bicycle and propped it against a tree so that he could have a good look at it. Bone-Shaker was one mass of rust. The front mudguard was missing and the back one was only fastened on by one piece of wire. The tyres were so worn they were practically smooth and had patches all over the place, but the brakes still worked and the wheels did seem to be round. Warily he mounted, found that the saddle did not need adjusting, and pedalled gently for a few yards along the verge.

'I'll pump the back-tyre up a bit, and then I think it'll do,' he said when he dismounted. 'Bring the luggage over here!'

They began to get ready at once. Daniel folded the blanket two or three times to make a cushion for the luggage rack. He strung the hold-all behind the saddle and tied the haversack to the cross-bar.

'What are we going to do about Patapon?' Manou asked anxiously.

'Balance the cage on top of the hold-all and keep it steady between your arms. We shan't be going very fast in any case. . . . The worst job will be getting on to the bike without sending us all into the ditch.'

'We shall look a fine sight if we do overbalance!' Manou exclaimed.

They both began to laugh. Daniel was so pleased to own this comical piece of machinery, for it not only gave them freedom of movement but also protected them from inquisitive eyes. Two dusty children trailing down an empty road could not help but attract attention, but who would take any notice of a young cyclist carrying his younger brother on the pillion up and down the hills?

While his brother firmly held the bicycle, Manou succeeded at the third attempt in getting on to the pillion. Daniel handed him the cage and then gingerly cocked his left leg over the cross-bar. As he pushed on the pedal the shaky structure set off with a series of sinister creaks and groans as it was buffeted by the slipstream of the cars speeding out of the bend. The first five hundred yards were up a fairly stiff slope and as Daniel struggled up it he thought it would never end. At last in front of them the road began to sweep downhill and as the bicycle gathered speed they passed their first milestone – *Bordeaux 70 m.*

'We'll be there by tonight,' Daniel shouted excitedly. 'Tomorrow we'll be in the Landes and the night after that we'll be in Chiberta. Things really are starting to look up!'

Twenty miles farther on, beyond Barbezieux, his sufferings really began. The heat was unbearable and, although Daniel had tied his coat to the cross-bar, the sweat was soon pouring off his face. In places, the fine plane-trees which lined the main road disappeared, and then the tarmac seemed to stretch ahead endlessly, without a scrap of shade, shimmering in the heat. There was no more question of cycling up the hills. At each slope

Daniel had to dismount, push the heavy mass of old iron and urge on Manou who complained about anything and everything: his feet hurt, he was much too hot, the pillion cushion was hard, he was hungry or thirsty or sleepy.

'Keep walking!' Daniel was harsh. 'Or else I'll leave you and your Patapon behind. The cross-eyed man'll come after you and catch you both.'

The little boy would hurry on or else begin to snivel as he looked anxiously over his shoulder. But there was no sign of the snooper, although Daniel reflected with some bitterness that he could not be far away.

Although he worked like a Trojan and made only the shortest of halts, by five o'clock he had only covered thirty miles. They had just come through a little village called Montlieu after slogging it up a hill in the dust and fumes of the heavy lorries heading for Bordeaux. The two boys went a little farther to clear the last few houses and then collapsed in the shade of a sunken road leading off towards a dilapidated farmhouse. Manou greedily gobbled a bar of chocolate and what was left of the bread, but Daniel's mouth was too dry for him to swallow anything. He pushed on to the farm where an old skinflint sold him a pint of milk at well over the normal price. He made Manou drink three-quarters of it and was content to enjoy a few mouthfuls. This put him on his feet again. The sun was not so hot now: the road seemed to run level, and a breeze, with the smell of the sea in it, had begun to flutter the trees along the roadside.

'Can't we go on again?' Manou asked after a minute or two. Now he had had some food he was his cheerful self.

Daniel was just getting up, when he saw a wavering shape through the trees which screened them from the main road. It was the cross-eyed man! His face was purple, and he was wheeling a bicycle little better than their own. After his physical ordeal, Daniel was less inclined to take seriously the threat of the man who was sticking to their heels.

'It's all right!' he jeered. 'Here we are! Your legs are not too stiff, are they?'

In his fury, the other loosed a volley of swear-words which made the two jokers laugh all the louder. Then he swung an unsteady leg over the cross-bar and disappeared in the direction of Bordeaux, pedalling like mad.

'Up you get!' Daniel told Manou as he hoisted the Bone-Shaker off the ground. 'It's our turn now – we're going to chase *him* for a change!'

It was only boyish fun, but Daniel regained his second wind in this imaginary chase. It all seemed so much easier. There weren't so many hills, they were not so long nor so steep, and Manou on the luggage-rack seemed to have grown much lighter.

'You're not tired are you?' Daniel shouted, without looking round. 'You don't want to stop for a minute or two, do you?'

'No!' yelled Manou. He was wildly excited and was watching the road ahead like a hawk. 'Faster! Faster!'

Daniel was not concerned about winning this old crocks' race, he was just a little drunk with the fresh air and exercise. No matter what happened, he was going to bring Manou safely home and that was all that mattered. So, fiercely he pushed the pedals round, thinking how each turn of the wheels brought them closer to their goal, Chiberta, and the safety of the family circle waiting for them there. Come what may, he would have to keep going a little longer.

The sun was low on the horizon when, at seven in the evening, the Bone-Shaker swept at top speed across the bridge over the green waters of the Dordogne. That meant only another fifteen miles to Bordeaux. They had covered half that distance when slowly and silently the air hissed out of the front-tyre. The rim rang like a bell at the slightest bump, making Daniel slow up at first. However, he soon went off at top speed again, for what did one more rattle matter when the whole bicycle clanked like a load of old iron? Then it was the turn of the back-tyre to go just as they passed the cross-roads at Quatre-Pavillons. Manou gave a yelp of pain every time they went over a bump.

They turned one last corner and then swept down the long hill to Bordeaux, almost the last stage of the wanderers' sufferings. The Bone-Shaker gave up completely on the railway-bridge at La Bastide. In a flash the front wheel broke into eight pieces, the chain flew off and the luggage-rack collapsed on to the rear mudguard with a sharp crack. By some miracle, Daniel landed with both feet on the ground and Manou clinging to his shoulders. He still held the handlebars from which the frame dangled at the end of the brake-cables.

The splendid din made by the crash stopped passers-by, who formed a laughing, sympathetic group around the young travellers. Daniel did not waste any tears on the Bone-Shaker, a nightmare from which he was free at last. Manou, of course, was helpless with laughter.

'Come far?' asked an onlooker, his curiosity aroused by their sensational arrival.

'Paris!' Daniel answered proudly, appropriating the three hundred miles the student had covered before him.

The bicycle was in four pieces, but might still tempt a purchaser prepared to take a gamble. Daniel was just about to shove the heap of old scrap-iron into the side of the road, when out of the crowd came a baker's boy with a basket on his arm.

'You could mend that!' He spoke confidently. 'Put a good pair of tyres on her and she'd still be some use.'

'You're probably right, but I'm just not interested.'

'I'll buy it off you. How much do you want?'

Daniel was too honest to make money from what had been given to him.

'I offered a glass of lemonade in exchange for the bike,' he said, laughing, 'and I never thought I'd be taken up on it. You can have it for a bit of bread.'

'Here you are!' said the errand boy, slipping a long loaf, still warm from the oven, under Daniel's arm.

Both sides parted in mutual satisfaction. Daniel knew Bordeaux slightly, but, after the misadventures of the night before, he was suspicious of built-up areas and so they wended their way slowly down to the Garonne. There they followed the riverside until they were out of the suburbs. At a shabby café on the water's edge the owner herself served them two plates of thick soup for a mere nothing. Manou's jaw dropped at the sight of this dog-food – you could have stuck your spoon upright in it.

'Bit of a change from roast chicken at the Régina,' said the unsympathetic Daniel, 'but we'll make up for it when we get to Chiberta. Meanwhile you'd better get stuck into the soup and the bread – it'll fill the corners!'

Daniel cleared his plate in a daze of tired limbs and sleepy head. He paid the bill, slipped the remains of the bread into the haversack and shakily got their luggage together. He could think only of sleep.

'Where are we going to get a bed?' Manou yawned.

'Not in a bedroom,' Daniel answered, thinking gratefully that it was a warm summer evening with the promise of a fine night for homeless wanderers. 'Come on, we'll find somewhere to sleep, with running water laid on.'

Farther on, beyond a shallow cover in which old punts lay rotting in the mud, the riverside returned to open country. Beside the solid planks and piles of a landing-stage, stood a wooden hut with a caved-in roof, which must at one time have been used as a bathing-hut or a tool-shed. It was an isolated spot and the golden glow of the sunset had by now disappeared from the water. Daniel examined the shelter and saw that it was both clean and dry. It did not take him long to make a bed for Manou in the most sheltered corner with the straw lying on the floor. The little boy went straight to sleep rolled tightly in the blanket, his head resting on the red and grey hold-all and Patapon nestling in the hollow of his arm. He had gone out like a light.

Daniel piled the rest of the straw against his young brother and snuggled down in this bedding, his face turned towards the yawning cavity of the door. Exhausted though he was, all his senses were on the alert. A soft foot-fall made the planks of the landing-stage creak. Suddenly it stopped and then it began again all around them, now close now far away. Daniel listened for a few minutes, his heart beating in wild alarm. Then he closed his eyes with a smile. It was only the rising tide lapping against the piles. He could forget the cross-eyed man.

8

Bastille Day

THE first firework went off at day-break, awakening both the boys and the guinea-pig. Daniel and Manou looked at one another in alarm. There followed a string of small explosions, more like a car backfiring than a battle, while from the nearby suburb came cheerful shouts and gusts of laughter.

After a bit of mental arithmetic with the dates, Daniel to his great relief was able to announce,

'Of course, it's Bastille Day!'

This was quite enough for Manou, who went back to sleep immediately, but Daniel stretched his cramped limbs and poked his nose out of their shelter. There was not a soul anywhere near them. Two hundred yards upstream, a solitary fisherman was casting his line and his reel whirred in the still air.

The morning sunshine was bright, and there was a sparkle in the air which exhilarated Daniel as he went down the steps of the landing-stage to wash in the river. Camping had its advantages. It took longer to get Manou ready, but Daniel washed his brother's face and brushed his hair as carefully as he had done in the bathroom at the Hotel Régina.

'We aren't tramps,' he said, vigorously washing Manou behind the ears. 'If we're clean and tidy, we can go where we like and the police won't notice us.'

He had made up his mind to go straight through Bordeaux, catching a bus to the Porte de Talence if need be, but it was so pleasant to stroll along that by the time they had reached the centre of the town, his resolution had disappeared. They wandered slowly about the Allées de Tourny, where a disorderly crowd milled around the coach stops in a more cheerful version of the scene on the Esplanade des Invalides. Daniel chose a quiet little café for their morning chocolate and when he had paid for it he had only two francs left. In a flash of inspiration he decided to risk them on a telephone call which might settle their difficulties in a few seconds.

'You never know,' he told Manou, 'if his boat hasn't been held up, Uncle Jérôme may be at the Villa Etchola by now. And even if he isn't, I've still a slight chance of catching the caretaker, Madame Bégou. She's almost sure to go into the house every two or three days to keep it tidy. If one or the other answers the phone, I'll be able to talk to them and tell them what's happened. It's only nine o'clock now, and Bayonne's only a hundred and twenty miles or so from Bordeaux so someone could be here by midday to fetch us in a car.'

'That would be lovely!' Manou exclaimed.

There was no call-box in the café. The phone itself was by the cash-desk, which rather embarrassed Daniel when he thought of all the fuss it would make to put the call through. However, the proprietor asked for the number at once, and a few minutes later called the boy over.

'They've got through for you,' he said. 'Take the receiver, you won't have long to wait.'

Over the crackle of the line, Daniel could hear the desperate shrilling of the bell in the empty house.

'There's no reply from Biarritz, caller,' said the Bordeaux operator after a little while. 'Would you like me to try again later?'

'No point, thanks all the same,' said Daniel. He suddenly felt very deflated.

His legs ached from the exertions of the day before, but he began to wish he still had the Bone-Shaker.

'Up you get!' he said roughly to Manou. 'There's not going to be a car, and there's no point in waiting around here. I don't even know what I'm going to do about lunch.'

'H . . . has all your money gone?' stammered his young brother.

'More or less. I've only got a couple of francs left, but that doesn't mean we'll have to beg.'

He looked at Manou out of the corner of his eye. His small brother had grown a lot more tough in the last two days, sharing all the hardships their crazy wanderings had brought them.

'There's only one way out,' Daniel said solemnly, to test him. 'We'll have to cook Patapon over a camp-fire and eat him with a bit of salt. He'd keep us going until tomorrow.'

Manou was outraged. He snatched his hand away and tried to escape into the crowd. Daniel caught him up in three strides.

'Come on, I was only joking. Don't take everything so seriously, you old stupid! We aren't over the worst part yet, so you'll have to keep your chin up.'

Manou seemed unusually eager to hold Daniel's hand again.

'That man's here again,' he whispered. 'There he is, behind us. And he's lost his bicycle, too.'

His brother couldn't imagine what he was talking about. That particular worry had vanished with the night.

'What man?' he asked, half turning round.

'The man with the funny eyes, of course,' said Manou. 'He doesn't look as though he's had a wash either, he's even grubbier than he was yesterday afternoon.'

Then Daniel saw the snooper, leaning up against a newspaper-kiosk. The slump of his body told all too clearly how desperately tired he was, while his threadbare suit, his dusty shoes and his unshaven chin made you almost sorry for him. A sudden gust of rage made Daniel's face flush, but the feeling passed as, in spite of it all, he began to admire the skill of their shadower and the persevering, faultless knack he had of following so long a trail and giving himself away so seldom.

'Pooh! He's not worth getting upset about!' he said, leading Manou away. 'It doesn't matter where we go, he'll be behind us like a guardian-angel. I'm beginning to get used to him anyway, so when we walk past him, don't look away, but give him a nice smile instead. Might just as well be polite to him, even if he is such a nuisance.'

The snooper's eyes crossed in an agonized expression and Manou never did know if his smile had done him any good.

'We'll sit down on that bench and rest until it's ten o'clock,' Daniel said. 'Then I'll buy the bread for today and we'll go and see if it's easier to get a lift to Chiberta from Bordeaux than it was outside Angoulême.'

They had been sitting in the sunshine for some five minutes, alone in the noise and bustle of the crowd, when two people came and parked themselves quietly at the other end of the bench. Daniel was repacking his bag. He was having a hard job folding the blanket into a less awkward shape in order to stow it away, so for the moment he paid no attention to the newcomers. A boyish voice overlaid by a slight English accent made him prick up his ears.

He looked up sharply and so did Manou. The other couple did the same, and all four stared at one another. Daniel was facing a boy of his own age, slightly more sun-burned than he, wearing shorts and a very smart blazer, while Manou's eyes met those of a small boy who

was as like him as a brother. From his nearby position under a tree the snooper watched the sudden doubling act of the Quint children. He rubbed his eyes in surprise.

Meanwhile the four boys were glaring at one another like strange dogs, until the two youngest began to grin and their elders copied them. Shy hullos were followed by commonplace remarks about the weather and the strike.

'We've been on our own for the last five days,' Daniel confessed, laughing. 'We're heading for Chiberta. So far we've made it on foot, by lorry, bus and bicycle and I shouldn't be surprised if we don't end up astride a donkey! . . . What about you?'

'We're not going anywhere.' Daniel's swarthy opposite number looked depressed. 'And the longer we're on our own, the better it'll be for both of us!'

As Daniel raised his eyebrows at this, a crazy idea flashed across his mind. This was all the other boy would say. He turned his back on them, at the same time giving his young brother a tap on the ankle.

'You wouldn't be the Jackson-Villars boys, would you?' Daniel asked.

It had been a shot in the dark, but the elder of the strangers started anxiously.

'Not so loud!' hissed the swarthy boy, hunching his shoulders defensively.

A strained face stared at Daniel.

'How did you guess? Yes, I'm Steve Jackson-Villars, and this is Benny.'

'For the last couple of days they've been chasing Manou and me,' Daniel answered dully, 'all because of this scrap of paper.' And he showed him the cutting from Madame

Julie's paper. 'I should be cursing you. I don't know how you're going to get out of it, but meanwhile you've landed us in a fine old mess.'

Steve looked at the photograph in the paper and read the article, while Daniel gave a brief account of their adventures. At first the group sat in tongue-tied amazement, and then they all burst into a howl of laughter. Even the worst moments were quickly forgotten.

'Well, we're all four of us in the same boat!' Steve exclaimed jokingly.

'Oh no, we're not!' Daniel protested. 'You ran away from home. That's different. Manou and I are just lost children.'

As the sun rose higher in the sky, the shadow cast by the trees closed gradually round the bench, turning it into a private place with almost the friendly security of a home. Manou had opened the door of his bird-cage to let Benny stroke Patapon and the two small boys chirped away, happily ignoring their elders. Steve dropped all affectation to take Daniel into his confidence.

'I didn't run away with Benny just for the fun of it,' he said bitterly. 'Don't you believe it! It's tough if you love your father or your mother, or your brother or your sister, and then they die. Misfortune can come so quickly. But it's far worse if they're still alive and yet as good as dead because they've had a row and one goes one way and the other another. Life's not too bright for children once their parents decide to separate – and that's what's happened to ours! One of these fine days I'm going to find myself all alone with my father in New York, while Mummy and Benny'll be on the other side of the globe in Mexico, Rome or Sidney. Needless to say, they won't ask their children what they think about it! We'll only see each other again for a couple of minutes every six years or so . . . that'll be fun, won't it?'

'Well?' asked Daniel, impressed.

'Well, I made my own sort of protest. The family often tells me I'm as wild as my Irish cousins – and they're dead right! There's only one way of bringing Mummy and Daddy together again before it's too late, and that's to do a dramatic disappearing act. At the moment things couldn't be worse. Daddy's up to his eyes in business and is away most of the time, Mummy wants to get back into films and runs round to all the festivals. Luckily that doesn't stop them adoring us. I used that . . .'

'Got it all worked out, then?'

'Of course I had. I won't say our old Uncle at Chantilly helped me, but he knew when to turn a blind eye. I took Benny – he was game – and off we went. Things started happening pretty quickly after that! Mummy and Daddy each had to fly about three or four thousand miles to get back to Paris. They put a stick of dynamite under the police and everyone was after us. Meanwhile Benny and I have spent the last six days quite quietly on a busy camping-site at Royan, without a soul recognizing us! Benny was quite all right. We slept under canvas and the camp restaurant was pretty good. But now the fun's gone on long enough and I'm beginning to wonder what's going to happen next.'

As he spoke he did not disguise his weariness. This odd confession left Daniel silent. He understood Steve's motives completely – the fear he had of his parents' absolute separation – but he was less ready to condone the flight of the two hot-heads, calculated in advance to force the hand of their parents by playing on their distress.

'The first thing to do,' he said quietly, 'is to set your parents' minds at rest. Send them a telegram.'

'I'd thought of that,' Steve replied, shaking his head. 'But what I'm frightened of is that we'd have a mob of police and reporters on our necks six hours after we'd sent it off. Mummy and Daddy are too rich and too well known – it's always so difficult for people like that!'

'Would you like me to send it for you?' Daniel suggested. 'It would be wiser, anyway. I'll do it in my name, give them only the barest details and tell them that you'll be writing.'

'And then?'

'You're stuck here anyway because of the strike, so why don't you come on with us to Chiberta? You and your brother'll be safe there while we wait and see what happens. It'll take us two or three days to get there, but that'll give time for things to take their course and, maybe, you'll avoid your biggest worry.'

Steve smiled at his new friend; the idea obviously attracted him.

'What are we going to do if someone collars us on the way? It could happen, you know.'

'Not necessarily. They're looking for two boys, not four. That'll fool them!'

With the slightest nod of his head he pointed out the cross-eyed man, pacing slowly round his tree and watching them furtively.

'We've been shadowed since we left Paris,' he added, dropping his voice. 'But you can bet he isn't a policeman, or we'd never have got as far as this. I just don't know what he's up to.'

At first Steve seemed rather scared, but Daniel's smile soon reassured him.

'Meeting you like this will only put him farther off the scent. If he wants to go on shadowing us, well, let him. As far as we're concerned, the main thing for us is to get away from here as fast as we can.'

'I'd a fair amount of money to start with,' said Steve,

'but I've only twenty francs or so left now. Is that going to be enough to get us to Chiberta?'

'It might just be enough for two, but not for all four of us.'

'Well, then you must all have lunch with me!' Steve exclaimed with magnificent abandon. 'In a restaurant.'

'You'd do better to keep the money in case we need it in the next few days,' was Daniel's careful advice. 'You see I've only two francs myself.'

Manou's and Benny's heads had jerked up at the sound of lunch and they watched their elder brothers eager-eyed. Neither uttered a word, but their eyes were eloquent advocates for the instant sacrifice of Steve's twenty francs.

'Let's take a vote on it,' said the latter, resigned by now to abject poverty. 'Here, you two! Who's for lunch?'

In perfect unison both small boys raised their hands. Neither Steve nor Daniel stirred; they worried about the morrow.

'Patapon needs his meals like anyone else,' Manou said sharply. '*He* should be given a half vote anyway. . . . Do you want your lunch, Patapon?'

There was a plaintive squeak from the bird-cage.

'Right!' Steve exclaimed. 'That settles it. We'll blue the twenty francs, and no arguments afterwards!'

They all scrambled to their feet. The only luggage the Jackson-Villars had was a blue and a red beach-bag, which made them look like young holiday-makers. The first thing they did was to go to the main Post Office at the end of the Cours de l'Intendance.

Daniel went in alone, leaving the others outside while he composed a telegram in which, in twelve words, he tried to express the love of the runaways for the parents and their sorrow for what they had done. Short though it was, in writing this simple message for somebody else Daniel gained not only personal satisfaction, but also the feeling that their path to Chiberta would be smoothed.

Having done this, the light-hearted band set out to explore the Allées de Tourny for a restaurant with a menu at five francs inclusive of tips and as much bread as you wanted. Like a flock of vultures they swooped on a café terrace festooned with flags and bunting where the Fourteenth of July menu offered the four young gluttons a wide choice of good food, and plenty of it, to satisfy their hunger.

The first basket of bread melted like snow. The plate of *hors d'œuvres* danced three times round the table and returned, clean, to the kitchen. In the twinkling of an eye, the *vol-au-vents*, oozing chopped meat and mushrooms, were speared, knifed, forked and spooned away. The girl at the cash-desk, the head-waiter and his five underlings in their white aprons watched the locusts in amazement. Then, with no delay, the national dish – steak and fried potatoes – appeared on the table. The four paused, but only to express their satisfaction.

'Excitement makes you hungry!' Manou chirruped as he stuffed Patapon with radish-leaves.

They returned to the attack with knife and fork and bread to sop the gravy up. *No charge for extra potatoes* was boldly underlined on the menu, but when two more large plates of chips had vanished the management realized that their promise had been a little rash. The chef in his white hat peered anxiously through the serving-hatch, but Steve and Benny were squinting at the cheese-board by now. An over-confident waiter was stupid enough to put it on their table and they cleared it with renewed appetite, like soldiers on the march.

The other customers kept up a running commentary and cheered them on. All the tables were full, including a rickety affair on a platform near the entrance. At it sat a lonely diner – none other than the cross-eyed man himself! In his race to keep up with the four boys he picked up the salt in mistake for the pepper on which his right eye was fixed and absent-mindedly sprinkled it into his glass of wine.

The Quint-Jackson-Villars team beat the snooper by the length of the field, gobbling up a fair-sized raspberry tart in record time. Steve paid the bill. There was no change, so out they all dashed, bubbling over with the joke and the feast they had enjoyed.

It was the worst time of day. The streets of Bordeaux were like an oven, and Daniel thought the agony of the day before was about to begin again. They made their way on foot as far as Talence, keeping in the shade of the houses. The south-bound traffic still flowed past, but much less thickly because of the holiday, and anyway it is not at all easy to find four seats in the same car. Daniel and Steve took it in turns to make the hallowed gesture of the hitch-hiker, their thumbs sweeping in the direction in which they imagined Chiberta to lie.

They were just out of the suburbs when the driver of a Citroën 4CV offered them a couple of seats. These they stoically refused. They had been friends for the past two hours and they were not going to risk losing each other at the very outset. In any case, for the first time Daniel felt free of the nagging fear which had set him and Manou on the run. He did not bother to decide whether this was because he was now the companion of two real criminals or whether it was because home and safety were so close ahead, still less did he bother about the difficulties which were still in front of them.

In single file they walked along the verge and had gone a little over six miles by four o'clock that afternoon. The two youngsters were lagging, but pride drove them on, for each hoped secretly that the other would be the first to give in. Past Gradignan the pine-forests began to close in on the road, and there Steve and Daniel decided to have a long rest. No longer even bothering to glance at the stream of vehicles thundering past, the boys sat down on the top of the bank with the good smell of the pine-trees in their nostrils. The far-sighted Daniel shared out the remains of the bread and a bar of chocolate, and gave Benny and Manou a good sip of lemonade.

'I'm sticking here,' Steve announced, lying on his back in the grass. 'The two kids can take it in turns to watch the road.'

'You first,' Daniel told Manou. 'If you see a car coming in the distance that looks as though it hasn't many people in it, give us a shout. We'll lie down in the middle of the road to make it stop.'

He only said this as a joke, for both the older boys had by now given up hope. Steve had gone straight to sleep: Daniel tried to keep an eye open to watch the youngsters, but the soft grass betrayed him, and he dropped off to dream of the cross-eyed man. Ten minutes later he woke with a start.

'The car's here!' The two smaller boys were dancing with joy. 'The driver's such a nice man, he'll take us all. Do hurry!'

Steve and Daniel sat up in tongue-tied amazement at this miracle. Right under their very noses was parked a vintage sports-car, its wheels giving the canary-yellow coachwork a terrific clearance from the road, its engine ticking over with a gasping roar. The driver was a small and bespectacled young man in a flowered shirt and white drill slacks. He waltzed self-importantly round the machine, polishing the wind-screen, testing the tyre-pressure and listening to the engine-note through the slits in the bonnet.

'You're not pulling our legs, are you?' Steve cried. 'You really will give us a lift, won't you?'

'Of course I shall!' The young man beamed. 'I've friends expecting me at Saint-Jean-de-Luz this evening, so I'll drop you off at Bayonne on the way. If the wheels don't fall off my old bus, we'll be there by eight. But you've got to be ready for anything in this old crock!'

He roared with laughter as he flung open both the doors.

'You'll be my first passengers, too!' he added proudly. 'This is going to be a splendid trip. You can say what you like, but a car does make a man of you!'

In a flash they had picked up their luggage and were grouped around the vintage car. Steve got into the back seat with Manou and Benny, while Daniel sat next to the driver, who seemed more excited by the prospect of giving them a lift than the boys themselves were at getting one. Daniel himself was wondering by what miracle the car could have come all that way from Bordeaux without picking up half-a-dozen hitch-hikers. He soon knew the answer.

'It's my first trip, too!' the young man admitted with a simper. 'It's a sort of celebration for passing my test. I'd failed it ten times, and only got my licence yesterday. . . . It's not that I'm worse than anyone else, but I get so flustered if I've got an examiner beside me. But I must have worn them down in the end, eh?'

The boys sank back luxuriously. The old-fashioned upholstery was as comfortable as ever, and they were all right. Their dashing driver, meanwhile, put the car into gear and let in the clutch. With a grinding roar the sports-car leaped backwards.

'Oh dear!' The young man was quite unperturbed. 'I shoved the gear lever too far. First isn't far away. Let's try again.'

One false step did not depress the passengers. The vintage car jerked off – in the right direction this time – stones flying up from the wheels.

'Chiberta, here we come!' yelled the trio on the back seat.

Daniel's lips tightened once more.

9

The Empty Train

UNDER its aged bonnet, the yellow sports-car retained a powerful engine that its driver had still to learn to control. To his alarm, Daniel watched the speedometer flicker up – fifty . . . sixty . . . seventy!

'I'm still only in third!' the young man announced ecstatically. 'Let's see how she does in fourth. . . . Clutch in . . . that's it! Now, gear hard down to the right . . . easy with the clutch . . . put your foot down, now, boy, and off we go again! . . . You all right in the back there?'

Steve and the two youngsters shrieked their delight. The needle of the speedometer tipped the eighty mark, the whole car shuddered and the engine beat was like a trip-hammer. Daniel did not mind the way in which the mile-stones sped past, but the over-confidence of their driver gave him more than a twinge of doubt. It was a great relief that the road through the Landes ran straight and uniform for mile after mile with never an awkward stretch for their learner-driver. The latter never stopped talking. His head revolved like a weather-vane. He took not a scrap of notice of the road ahead, let go of the steering-wheel to gesticulate, passed other vehicles on the right and the left and no matter what enormity he perpetrated kept up a running commentary interrupted with hoots of laughter.

'Brake on . . . she's slowing up . . . clutch . . . carefully now, into third . . . into third. . . . Blow the horn to warn that fool on the bicycle! . . . Did you see how he got out of the way! . . . Change up! . . . Easy as pie . . . come on, old

girl, you'll soon knock off those hundred and fifty miles if you keep up fifty all the way!'

He kept turning round every other minute to see the admiration of his passengers. From the bonnet seeped a cloud of sickly, evil-smelling smoke. Their crazy driver did not even slow up when he went through a village. As a result they ran over a couple of geese at La House, while at Bellême a cackling hen whizzed over the top of the windscreen like an eagle and at Lamothe a tabby cat by some miracle went between the wheels. Steve and the two youngsters kept the score, laughing until they cried.

The first corner loomed in the distance, but the vintage car rushed into it at the same wild speed. The young man was pushing the accelerator through the floor. Tyres

screamed, the car skidded wildly to the left, narrowly missing a motor-scooter coming in the opposite direction, bounced over the verge and ended up with its nose buried in the bank.

'Nothing to worry about!' the lunatic exclaimed as he jumped out. 'The old girl just got the bit between her teeth, that's all! I've got her well in hand, but she sometimes has these fits.'

Daniel got out, too, to see what was the damage. One headlamp had come adrift, the left mudguard was badly dented and the front bumper was twisted into a 'W'. Daniel expected an outburst of lamentation, if not a long delay or even a curt farewell from their benefactor. Nothing, however, could quench his beginner's enthusiasm: his one thought was to keep going as fast as he could and as long as his old sports-car held together. He bellowed with laughter once he saw that it was a matter of a few scratches and that no vital damage had been done. He tore the head-lamp right off and chucked it into the boot, and kicked the dents out of his mudguard. The front bumper was taken care of by jerking the car into reverse and leaving it like some trophy in the hedge.

'Wasn't much use anyway! Get rid of a hundredweight of old iron and that'll help lighten the ship a bit. . . . Let's go! . . . Changes gear as smooth as silk. . . . And you just listen to that engine note. . . . Like a Merlin. . . . For future reference, kids: a good car, a driving-licence, a full tank and the open road in front of you – it's heaven! . . . Hullo! Hullo! What are those two cows doing in the middle of the road?' he added with a bloodthirsty chuckle.

'No! No! No!' The boys came to their senses and protested loudly. 'They're too big.'

This saved the cows, but it did not save their milk. It must have curdled in the slip-stream as the car whistled past them. Four miles farther on one of the rear tyres burst and the old crock slithered to a halt on the grass verge.

'A flea-bite!' the maniac exclaimed. 'I've a couple of spares. Everybody out! I'll show you how to change a wheel. . . . The jack's under the back seat. Give me all that clobber. No need to help. I'll have the job done in two minutes!'

The repairs took half an hour. It was as good as a music-hall turn – the idiotic young man in a fever of impatience breaking everything, getting it all the wrong way round and laughing even louder than Manou. In the end he roared off, leaving the jack and the old wheel on the road-side. Daniel took good care not to remind him, since he would have needed to make a perilous U-turn and the ditches along the road at that point were a good three feet deep.

Curses and cat-calls accompanied the old crock on her wild flight across the Landes. At Belin the whole village was dancing on the square to a brass band ensconced on a decorated platform right alongside the road. The way was clear, but as ill-luck would have it, just as they were coming up, another car turned in from a side road. Their inexperienced driver turned the steering-wheel too violently and the car brushed against the platform, which slightly overhung the pavement. There was a crisp sound of ripping canvas and the awning split in two to reveal the musicians sitting there and blowing like men possessed. The dancers protested angrily but, instead of putting on his brakes, the young man accelerated. The old crock snapped off one of the struts of the platform, knocked down one of the poles which carried the decorations in the square, and went on its way trailing from the windscreen a long streamer of red, white and blue paper.

Drunk with speed, the young man had eyes only for the road swallowed up by the wheels of his car. The speedometer needle reached the eighty mark once more and slowly swung beyond it.

'I'll try and see if I can get her up to ninety!' he shouted suddenly, much to the alarm of Daniel and Steve. 'What about it? . . . The man I bought her from swore the old girl could do it.'

Luckily two motor-cyclists in black helmets and leather leggings loomed up behind them as though by magic, closed in on the old car and forced the budding Graham Hill to slow up. The car stopped in a cloud of smoke. The boys kept quiet, but the driver was as cheerful as ever and did not seem in the least disturbed by the arrival of the police. One of them dismounted and examined the vintage car with horror.

'We've booked you for four traffic offences in the last three miles,' he said severely. 'Let's have a look at your driving-licence, my lad!'

'Here it is, I got it yesterday.'

With a sweeping gesture which took in the road ahead, the old car and the boys huddled on the back seat, he added with pride,

'My first trip, my first car and my first passengers. Isn't it just wonderful?'

'Wonderful!' the policeman icily agreed, pulling a leaf from his note-book. 'And here's your first summons! I hope you stay alive long enough to pay the fine!'

Then he turned to the panic-stricken children.

'Wouldn't you rather get out here, before the first crash completes the chain of firsts? You'd be more sensible if you did.'

The young man in glasses did not give them the chance to answer as he switched on the engine.

'We've got our eye on you!' the speed-cops both shouted. 'You go a bit slower and keep to your own side of the road, you idiot!'

But the warning was unnecessary. Whether it was the abrupt stop, or just the rough treatment it had received, it was soon obvious that something had been too much for the old engine. From under the bonnet came a dull, thumping sound, while the car moved forward jerkily in alarming clouds of sickening smoke.

'First breakdown?' Daniel inquired, looking at his neighbour out of the corner of his eye.

His remark eased the tension for them all, including their crazy driver, who really did not worry what happened on his first time out. The machine managed to crawl another five hundred yards and then gave up with one last terrific back-fire.

'Not to worry!' the young man called. 'Let the old girl

cool down. She'll start up again as good as new in five minutes' time. A good driver needs to keep his patience. This bus has done the Monte Carlo Rally three times, and she just loves speed. All we've got to do is wait till she's ready.'

'All we want her to do is the Chiberta Rally!' Daniel grumbled to himself.

Five minutes passed and the man tried the self-starter. Nothing happened: the engine did not even cough. The boys' faces fell, but the young man tried again. Still nothing happened, except that the whine of the self-starter grew weaker and weaker, gave one or two more groans and then packed up completely.

'All right, all right! The battery must be flat,' their driver managed to tell them through his laughter. 'We'll just have to use the starting-handle, that's all. . . . Let me have it; it should be under the back seat.'

Steve handed him the starting-handle and he came round to the front of the car, clumsily inserted it and began to swing it. But however hard he turned the handle, all the response the engine would make was a tired wheeze. It just refused to start. The young man stood up to recover his breath and to wipe off the sweat that poured down his face. As he did so he saw the four boys sitting in the car watching him. He suddenly threw the starting-handle into the ditch as though he had no further use for it.

'What a fool I am!' he said in a new fit of hilarity. 'If I had the four of you on the job I could soon get the car moving fast enough. Then, when I told you to, you could push even harder. I'd let in the clutch and the old girl would start to fire. . . . Get everything out!'

Unwillingly the boys removed themselves and their luggage from the car. Then they set their shoulders to it. Their joint strength started the old girl rolling slowly forward.

'Faster! Faster!' shouted the madman at the wheel. 'Faster! Faster!'

Daniel and Steve were nearly running, straining angrily against the back of the car in an effort to shift the huge machine.

Then it backfired and leaped forward, leaving the helpers standing at the side of the road. The young man fumbled with the controls, braking, sounding the horn, setting the windscreen-wipers going, switching on the headlamps, flicking the indicators and stabbing the accelerator in a way which made the exhaust pipe belch black smoke. Behind chased the boys, encumbered by the baggage from which they would not be parted.

'Heavens! I can't stop her,' the driving-ace called, turning round to stare at them in panic. 'Jump on to the running-board and I'll get the doors open for you.'

Steve and Daniel might have managed to make the jump, but the younger two were far behind already.

Gradually the gap between the car and its pursuers widened. The young man's attentions were divided between steering-wheel and gear-lever as he strove to hold back a sports-car that gathered speed every second. The old yellow car swerved from one side of the road to the other, nearly smashing into a car trying to overtake it. The boys stopped, breathless. Then, away in the distance, it was as though an invisible pair of spurs had been set into her sides. The old crock suddenly regained her speed and vanished in a cloud of dust down the long straight road.

Benny and Manou collapsed on their luggage in tears of disappointment. Daniel had to comfort them and get them on their feet again with the harsh truth. They might have made Chiberta that night, but only at the very real risk of sudden death!

'A pity,' Steve sighed. 'That was some adventure. Anyway, why complain? We've done over thirty miles in less than an hour. That old crock had its moments!'

The first sign-post said *Labouheyre ½ mile.*

'Let's head that way,' Daniel decided. 'We've got to find something to eat and some place to sleep. We're all tired.'

The two older boys tried their hand at hitch-hiking as they walked along, but most of the cars were belting along the straight at eighty miles an hour so their signals were ineffective. The wayfarers were sitting down for a moment in a line along the top of the bank when they were puzzled by a high-pitched buzz, as irritating as the whine of a mosquito, growing in intensity as it came nearer. The noise became even louder and when they could almost bear it no longer, round a gradual bend came a brand new power-cycle, heading at top speed for Labouheyre. The stiff figure of the cross-eyed man swept past them, clinging grimly to the handlebars, his long legs bent ridiculously over the pedals. He did not deign to answer their friendly greeting.

'He looks as though he's well away, too,' Benny remarked seriously. 'He's like that other crazy fool in the yellow car: the only way he'll be able to stop, is by running into a tree!'

Labouheyre was a large market-town tucked away in the middle of the pine-forests, on the main railway line from Bordeaux to Hendaye. It was as full of life as Belin, for the side-shows and the Fourteenth of July sports had drawn the young people from miles around. Daniel and Steve agreed that they ran no risk in that light-hearted atmosphere and that it was much better to finish on a gay note a day that had begun so well. Suddenly the youngsters regained all their energy as they mingled with the crowd cheering on the competitors in the sack race and those trying their luck at the Aunt Sally or the Lucky Dip.

Manou had a shot at the latter and was lucky enough to win an enormous stick of barley-sugar, which was divided between the four of them and eaten on the spot.

'This just takes the edge off your appetite,' Steve said scornfully. 'We need to set our sights a bit higher. . . . Look at that!'

He pointed to the tall pole at the other end of the market square. A crowd had gathered round it and the children had to push and shove to get to the front of the throng. The pole, a straight, slim pine-trunk, was a good fifty feet high, with a bunting-decked wheel at the top from which hung a tempting selection of foodstuffs. The crowd cheered the competitors who were waiting to climb for the huge smoked ham, the net full of bottles, the long sausage and, last but not least, the live goose, tied by its feet and exciting the greed of the crowd as it raucously croaked from its lofty perch.

'That ham is just what we need,' Steve whispered with a conspiratorial wink to Daniel. 'You any good at climbing?'

'I could get up there easy enough if it was a rope, but that pole's fairly thick at the base and they've greased the last few feet. Let the others have a go first, they'll clear the way for us.'

A dozen or so competitors stood at the foot of the pole, flexing their muscles. They had taken off their coats: some were barefoot, while others wore old rope-soled sandals. The first attempt was made by an athletic twenty-year-old. Up he went, slowly but surely, until, fifteen feet from the top, his hands reached the greasy section. He struggled on for another six feet, slipped back three, regained nine, reached in desperation for the neck of the goose and then came sliding down to fall in a heap at the foot of the pole amid the laughter of the onlookers.

'Who's next?' shouted the organizer.

A weedy youth with legs and arms like matchsticks

came forward. He did not look as if he could climb, and yet he shinned up with no apparent effort. The grease slowed him up slightly, but at last he reached the top and, to the cheers of the crowd, anchored himself so that he had plenty of time to make his choice. The goose defended itself with its sharp beak, so he chose the ham, which he unhooked with the greatest of ease and slid down to a burst of applause.

'That's one gone,' Daniel grumbled. 'And the best of the lot!'

Pitiless cat-calls greeted the failure, five feet from the top, of the next three climbers. The sixth was a small boy, all muscles, who reached the top, and, ignoring the goose, which was far too awkward a prize, picked the long sausage. Steve's and Daniel's mouths went dry. They could feel the reproachful eyes of their younger brothers. They hesitated.

'Let's wait a bit,' said Daniel. 'The pole won't be so greasy after another two or three tries.'

'No!' Steve retorted. 'I'm having a go now!'

All that was left was the net of bottles and the furious goose. Fighting like a demon, it pecked at half a dozen contestants, sending them slithering down the pole, sucking their bruised fingers. Now came Steve's turn. With the two youngsters yelling him on at the tops of their voices he easily made the first thirty feet and then inch by inch came level with the wheel. There was the goose waiting for him, its neck stretched out, all ready for the counter-attack. Steve tried to climb a little higher so as to catch it by its bound legs. Flapping its wings, the hefty fowl gave him a sharp nip in the seat of the pants. The pain made him loose his grip and down he slid. There was a hoot of laughter from the crowd.

'Your turn now,' the unfortunate told Daniel. 'There's hardly any grease left on the top of the pole, so it'll be easy for you. But watch out for that crazy bird. Leave it alone and try for the bottles. There are six of them, and someone's bound to offer us a good price for them.'

Daniel pushed his way to the front of the crowd, where the fourteenth contestant landed at his feet clutching the precious net of bottles.

'Come on, my lucky lads!' the organizer yelled to the crowd. 'The best prize is still at the top – a fine fat twenty-pound goose presented by the model farm at Castagnède. Who's going to win it?'

But not a soul was tempted. With a determined air, Daniel took off his coat and his shoes – come what might, he was resolved to have that goose for their dinner. A burst of cheering encouraged him as he gripped the pole firmly with his hands, while his socks gave him a good foothold on the slippery wood. Hardly realizing what he was doing, he was level with the wheel in less than half a minute. Below, Steve and the two young ones stood silent, mouths gaping and eyes fixed on him; above his head the goose gave an angry and ominous hiss.

Daniel tried to get a strong hold of the top of the pole so that he could catch the bird without taking too many risks. Just as he was doing so, the goose, straining on the end of the rope, caught him a cruel nip on his shoulder. The crowd roared. Angrily, Daniel let go of the pole with his left hand, and, stunning the bird with a sharp, defensive backhander, grabbed it by the neck and, without worrying what damage he might cause, pulled hard. Everything happened at once. There was a sinister crack and down came the top of the pole with its streamers, the wheel with its bunting, and the hissing goose with its wings flapping.

This was the debris surrounding him when Daniel came to again, now sitting on the ground, but still clutching the goose, which struggled feebly.

'You've well and truly won it!' the organizer said as everybody laughed. 'If it hadn't been for you we'd have had to get the fire-brigade, with their ladders, to take that brute down! Here's the basket. Shove it in. Don't bother to untie its legs or you'll have to catch it all over again.'

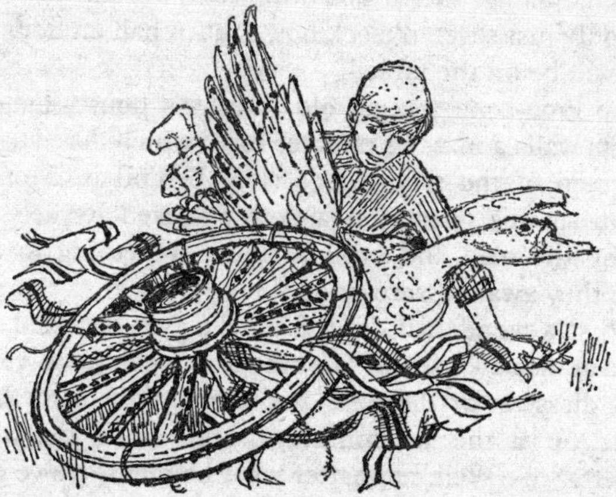

Manou, Steve and Benny were flushed with pleasure as they fought their way through the crowd to reach the champion, now being congratulated by the mayor and corporation. The goose was too dazed by its fall to put up a fight when they shut it in its basket.

'Can we eat it?' little Benny asked eagerly. 'How are we going to cook it?'

Daniel was beginning to think he had had the worst of the bargain, with Manou, Patapon, the luggage and now this awkward goose.

However, a stout, cheerful-looking man had been watching them with some amusement for the past few minutes, and now he came over, a broad grin on his face.

'My name's Castan,' he said, shaking Daniel by the hand. 'I own the restaurant over there – the Pine-cone.

How many of you are there? Four? . . . Right. If you'd like to swap your goose, I'll give you a meal you'll remember for a very long time. How about it, then?'

'Done!' said Daniel, handing over the prisoner in its basket.

'Come along, then,' said Monsieur Castan, delighted. 'It's only just seven o'clock now, but in half an hour your food will be on the table.'

The Pine-cone was an old forester's house, long and low, its walls a mass of rambler roses which flared against the green of the pine-woods close behind it. Monsieur Castan sat his guests on a flower-decked terrace overlooking the road and brought them something to drink while they awaited zero-hour.

'What a wonderful day!' Daniel's eyes sparkled as he stared at his new friends. 'For the last five days we've gone from disaster to disaster, yet every time something's turned up at the last minute to help us on the way to Chiberta. . . . Well, no matter what happens, we've got to be there by tomorrow night.'

'I simply can't take risks,' Steve objected. 'It was bad enough just now in all that crowd, and your cross-eyed man can't be far away.'

'The cross-eyed man has got nothing to do with *us* now,' Daniel teased him. 'We're only too glad to let you have him. Do what you like with him!'

Prompt on his cue, from the distance came the wavering whine of the power-cycle as it wandered up and down the narrow streets of the market-town or bumped over the paths through the surrounding forest. Steve shook his head; he did not want to take this threat seriously.

At half-past seven, just as had been promised, two waitresses came bustling out to the famished guests, and the feast began. Lunch in Bordeaux had gloriously stuffed their stomachs, but all the excitement of the afternoon had emptied them once again, and there was no hanging back. Every now and then Monsieur Castan would come out to make sure his guests were not choked by his fish soup, the eggs, onions, tomatoes and long red peppers of his *piperade*, or his stuffed chicken. By the third course his anxieties were running in the opposite direction and he was beginning to wonder if the goose was not going to prove too costly! To prevent further expense, he had the gluttons served with a sickly concoction of pastry and almonds, bursting with crystallized fruits and cream. This was enough even for the greediest.

Daniel began to worry about where they would sleep.

'We're right next door to the forest and there are masses of farms round about,' said Steve, 'and we'll be unlucky if we don't find an empty hut or an odd corner in a barn.'

They were full to bursting as they staggered out, rewarding Monsieur Castan with their broad grins. Daniel led the way as the little group made off down a sandy track which vanished into the forest. Two hundred yards away from the village, and they were in the depths of the woods, all around them the trunks of the tall pines scarred by the axes of the resin-tappers. Suddenly Steve spotted a little hut. Its door was secured only by a twist of wire.

'If we shove those tools to the back,' he said, 'there'll be enough room for the two kids. You and I can sleep outside the door on a thick bed of pine-needles.'

Daniel and Steve at once began to set the place to rights, while Manou and Benny, who had freed Patapon for a run in the woods, chased him with screams of delight.

Suddenly Manou began waving his arms in excitement.

'Come on!' he shouted. 'Oh, do hurry! We've found something much better!'

Steve and Daniel went to see what it was, and there,

beyond the trees, the railway-line sliced its way straight through the forest as far as the eye could see. Just a little way along the line was a level-crossing, beyond it a tiny country station with deserted platforms, and beyond that a row of carriages standing in a siding. It was an entire passenger-train, lacking only its engine!

'You could sleep a couple of thousand in that!' Daniel roared.

'The trains aren't running, so we might as well use them for something! Nobody from the village can see us getting in and we'll sleep in the lap of luxury in there. Hurry up and bring the luggage!'

They circled round through the forest to approach the train unseen.

'Let's travel First!' Steve laughed. 'It won't cost us any more.'

They chose adjoining compartments in the middle of a carriage, one for the Quints, the other for the Jackson-Villars. While the corridors resounded under the thunderous footfalls of the youngsters, Daniel explored the toilets. There was no water in the first one he came to, but when he turned on the tap in the second, out trickled a flow of cloudy water, which had stood tepid since the fatal stop on 11 July.

'Come and have a wash!' he called to the others. 'We've got everything here – even running hot water!'

Steve was removing cushions from other compartments to make his own bed more comfortable. The windows of the corridor looked out on to the forest, so Daniel pulled them all down and soon the clean scent of the pine-woods had freshened the stuffy atmosphere created by three days' standing in the blazing sun.

After they had all washed and Benny and Manou had been put to bed, Steve and Daniel took advantage of the deepening twilight to reconnoitre the whole of the abandoned train. The wanderers should have a peaceful night, for there was not another soul aboard.

'What about the guard's van?' Steve suggested. 'I'll bet the cross-eyed man's in there!'

By ten o'clock, they were all fast asleep, cradled by the murmur of the forest, gentle as distant surf.

10

Blast-off

DANIEL'S dream could hardly have been more pleasant. He was in a fairyland where trains were running far and fast, and if they stopped they started again almost at once. Grandfather had booked seven luxurious sleepers and the whole family was speeding towards Chiberta at ninety miles an hour. In the first sleeper were Granny and Grandfather, the latter scribbling out future 'movement orders'; back from England, in No. 2, were Mummy and Daddy; Manou and Daniel were stuffing away an enormous meal in No. 3, to compensate for their recent privations; in No. 4 Uncle Jules and his Italian wife lay swathed in bandages, their two offspring snoring away like steam-engines in No. 5; in No. 6 sat Uncle Jérôme, newly-returned from Africa, with his tame gorilla and his hunting rifles, while in No. 7 (animals only), little Patapon berthed with the fat goose from Labouheyre, which had taken a great liking to his conqueror. Needless to say, the cross-eyed man, disguised as a ticket-collector, promenaded the corridor with such a fearsome squint that he mistook the exit for the lavatory door and fell out on to the track with a tremendous crash.

Daniel laughed so much that he woke himself up. He sat up and stared. It was broad daylight and the train was running along at top speed. Their train, too! Beyond the blind, the monotonously forested landscape flashed past.

He rubbed his eyes hard. Was he still dreaming? Of course not. This was the very same compartment they had commandeered the evening before in the station of Labouheyre. There were the extra cushions, and their dusty shoes lay in evidence on the rack. Still their wanderings traced a destined, if unknown, course. An express train roared past them in the opposite direction, buffeting the half-open window of the empty train. The rail strike must be over! The rattle of the wheels had not woken Manou. There was an angelic smile on his face and no doubt he was involved in as extraordinary a dream as his elder brother had been.

Quietly Daniel opened the door and peered down the corridor in both directions. The coach still seemed completely empty. All was not yet lost; quite the contrary, in fact, if the train was making for the rail depots at Bayonne or Hendaye. Their adventure seemed to be ending in a glorious joke. He gave a short sharp rap on the door of the neighbouring compartment and slid it half open.

'All tickets, please!' he barked in the deepest voice he could manage.

Steve and Benny were so sound asleep that they nearly tumbled off their seats at this sudden awakening. Daniel doubled up with laughter.

'Wow! The train's running,' Steve said in ecstasy. 'How long have we been under way?'

'I don't know,' said Daniel. 'I've only just woken up myself.'

'What are we going to do?

'What can we do? Let it run. All the same, we'd better make sure we're going the right way. All we need do is watch out for the next little village and read the name of the station as we go through. Pull up your blind a bit and look out on that side; I'll go out into the corridor and watch the other side.'

The clatter of points warned them that they were approaching a station. Daniel crouched down, his head level with the bottom of the window. Station buildings flashed past.

'Morcenx!' he shouted as he stood up. 'We're heading straight for Bayonne!'

He went back and shook Manou. His younger brother surfaced from sleep with a flushed and disgruntled face.

'Let me sleep a bit more,' he whispered wearily. 'It's still dark.'

'Up you get!' shouted Daniel, wildly excited. 'Can't you feel the train's moving? We'll be in Chiberta in two hours!'

'Well, wake me up later, then,' Manou grunted coolly.

And he turned over and went back to sleep as though nothing at all had happened. Daniel let him be. Manou needed to make up for the discomfort of the two previous nights. Instead, Daniel fell upon the Jackson-Villars once more.

'Keep the blinds down in both compartments and show yourselves as little as possible,' he told Steve. 'It's easy for someone to use the phone and it would be silly to let ourselves be caught by an over-enthusiastic porter at the other end. I shan't stop worrying about Manou and the pair of you until we're really home.'

The shunting engine pulling their train was no crack locomotive trying to beat the world speed record on this particular stretch of line through the Landes. All the same, it kept up a fair pace which sent the fresh air blowing through their carriage. Little station after little station slid past. Daniel counted four of them. They were isolated in the desert of trees and their names meant nothing to him. Then the forest began to thin, more and more houses, closer and closer together, began to appear in the distance, and the train started to slow down slightly. Then a huge board announced in red letters – *Dax ½ m.*

'If only our train keeps going,' the two elder boys repeated as they nervously paced the corridor.

They looked at the railway map in the compartment.

'Look!' Daniel said anxiously. 'There's a linc branching off from Dax. If the train turns left, I expect we'll land up in Pau or Tarbes – and that will be the end of us!'

The train went through the station at Dax without stopping, swung away to the right and then picked up speed again.

'Saved!' Daniel exclaimed. 'Only another hour and our journey's over.'

'I'm hungry,' said Benny.

Daniel went to fetch the haversack in which, squirrel-like, he had saved at the end of each day's journey whatever scraps he could put aside for an emergency. There were dry crusts, squares of chocolate, sweets, biscuits, and the bottle of lemonade which he had been sensible enough to refill with water at the restaurant in Labouheyre. At the sound of eating Manou woke up as fast as if a bomb had exploded under his bed, and the four of them shared a snack in the Jackson-Villars compartment. The biscuits were stale, the crusts as hard as wood and the chocolate sticky and black with dust, but the wind of freedom made these scraps taste like a banquet.

The train kept up a good speed and the watchers read out the names of the stations as they passed. The names did not mean a thing to the boys, but each was greeted with cheers since it marked another stage miraculously nearer the delights and the peace of Chiberta. Beyond Saint-Vincent-de-Tyrosse, the forest with its resinous pines closed in again, but now a new intoxicating freshness in the air told them that the sea was not far away. For seven or eight miles the railway ran alongside the main road to Bayonne and although it was barely seven o'clock there was plenty of traffic glittering in the rising sun. Their train was moving faster than the cars and the boys enjoyed being on the winning side after all their rebuffs of the day before.

Then the line made a vast curve through Vieux-Boucau, and there suddenly was the mouth of the River Adour with Bayonne in the distance, its houses clustering under the shadow of the cathedral.

'We're nearly there,' Daniel said as he raised the blind so that they could see the whole view. 'Our only trouble will be getting off the train. If it stops right in the middle of Bayonne station, we're bound to have some explaining to do.'

'Maybe the ticket-collectors are still on strike,' joked Steve. 'But the only thing to do is to get out before we reach the station.'

As he said this, the brakes began to grind and the train slowed down to a walking pace. They were travelling along an embankment dropping down to the riverside factories, docks and warehouses. Then the brakes screeched again and a few seconds later the train came to a complete standstill. Daniel was careful to see if all was clear on the other, the corridor side.

'I think we'll be all right for a few minutes.' He sounded pleased. 'Two or three trains have stopped in front of us and it'll take some time to clear the track. Grab the bags! We'll get out on the other side. There's only a bank to scramble up and then we're in the open fields. No one can touch us there. . . . Hurry!'

Everything was ready in a few minutes and the four stowaways tip-toed down the corridor, awed by the heavy silence which had descended on the stationary train. Steve peered this way and that as he opened the door and got down first to help the smaller boys out. Then Daniel handed the luggage down to him, still scared that they might have to face an angry tirade from the guard. His fears were soon set to rest.

'We aren't the only ones,' Steve called to him with a laugh. 'Take a look at this.'

When Daniel too got down he could not believe his eyes. Simultaneously, and all with the same idea, some fifty or sixty other stowaways were pouring out of the neighbouring carriages.

'The cross-eyed man was on the train!' Manou yelled. 'There he is, getting his cycle out of the guard's van!'

'Why should we hide from him?' Daniel said calmly. 'Ignore him. In five minutes' time we'll be slamming the door of the Villa Etchola in his face.'

The whole laughing, chattering crowd took a narrow cart-track winding away to the river, four happy boys at their heels. In less than fifteen minutes they were in Bayonne.

Daniel and Steve turned out their pockets and managed between them to raise the two francs they needed for four tickets to Chiberta on the Cinq-Cantons bus. Daniel sank back into his seat with a wonderful feeling of relief. Manou was beside him, fit and well, and chirpy as a sparrow. Together they had covered the five hundred miles of their journey. It had been hard going, but they had never faltered, and, what was more, they had taken under their wing two now-repentant runaways, whom they had rescued from disaster.

The bus-route to Biarritz ran along the broad avenue beside the sea, encircling the huge pine-wood in the midst of which Chiberta lay. Manou was very proud to be the only one who knew the district and he was delighted to tell the others about the places they passed.

'The bar of the River Adour is way behind us; you can't see it from here. That's the turning down to the race-course. . . . We're just going to pass the miniature golf-course at Jolifon. . . . The next stop is ours. At the turning to the Country Club. . . . I'll tell you when we get there.'

They had an occasional glimpse beyond the dunes of a sea as blue and as smooth as silk. Brilliant sunshine pierced the screen of pines to highlight the fresh paint of the houses and the bright colours of their gardens. People in holiday clothes strolled along the avenues and smart cars passed the bus, each with its load of young people and children in swim-suits.

'Here we are,' Manou called and jumped up from his seat. 'Don't forget the luggage! Everybody out!'

They followed the small boy as he strode up the avenue like a conqueror, his beloved Patapon crouching in the bird-cage that swung from his fist. On every side Daniel saw the dreams that had filled the last days of term at his dreary school in Besançon become realities. He was not disappointed. This was the very sunshine, the very blue sky, the soft yet bracing air of the little forest paradise where every house seemed to smile at you from behind its flower garden, and where every lawn was like an open-air sitting-room surrounded by untidy shrubberies. On the other side of the road was the lake of Chiberta, set around with smart villas whose lawns came right down to the shore, and overhung by the noblest pines in the forest. Canoes, kayaks and pedalos in many different colours cut the mirror-like surface that gleamed like a sapphire in the glorious sunshine.

'Here we are!' Manou called over his shoulder. 'The Villa Etchola's just on the other side of the cross-roads.'

At last Monsieur Quint's large villa appeared to the ecstatic gaze of the wanderers. There, behind the oleanders thick with blossom, was the long, low, yellow-ochre building crowned by a roof of blue tiles which sparkled like diamonds in the sun. The lawn was mown, the flowerbeds freshly watered, and the petunias cast their scent everywhere. Alas – the front gate was locked, the shutters on the house were closed and no footmarks disturbed the sanded garden paths. However, the Quint grandchildren were not downcast for long.

'So we *did* get here first after all!' Daniel exclaimed cheerily. 'We simply need someone to open the place up for us. . . . Where does Madame Bégou live?'

Only a moment away, as it happened, in the lodge of a vast house they glimpsed in the distance at the end of a landscaped garden. The good lady herself was sweeping her front doorstep. She recognized Manou at once and told him how pleased she was to see him looking so well.

'You're first, to be sure you are. I haven't heard a word from your grandfather, either, and I've been expecting them any day. . . . And did you come all this way all on your very own? You can blame this wretched strike for that. . . . Well, I'll find the keys and open the villa for you. . . . But first of all, have you had breakfast?'

'Only bread and water,' Manou answered.

'Come into my kitchen, then, I've some milk on the stove!'

It must have been at least the sixth free meal that the wanderers had enjoyed, for at each stage of their journey they had found a smiling Good Samaritan to help them. Meanwhile Daniel gave Madame Bégou a brief account of their adventures and tactfully introduced the Jackson-Villars as school-friends of his.

'Well, there's plenty of room at the Villa Etchola, that's one good thing!' Madame Bégou laughed. 'I'll make up the beds for you and I'll look after your meals until Madame arrives. Come with me, now!'

The white garden gate opened with a squeak. As soon as they were inside, Manou put the bird-cage down on the garden path and opened the door.

'We're home now!' he cried. 'Patapon can go free, now, wherever he likes in the house or the garden.'

Full of excitement the little creature ran on to the flowerbeds, while Daniel thought happily to himself, 'I could just as well say, Manou can go free now. All my troubles are over.'

It was not until early afternoon that the cross-eyed man put in an appearance. In the shade of the pines, Daniel and Steve were comfortably lying in two deck-chairs on the terrace, overlooking the junction with the main road. They were reading peacefully and chatting while Benny and Manou tracked the quicksilver Patapon through the shrubs at the other end of the garden. The distant whine of the power-cycle gave the older boys a warning and then the man himself came into sight, clinging to the machine as it swept round the corner, the stubble on his chin even longer and his face even more drawn. He dismounted, propped his cycle against a tree and came straight across the road to examine the Villa Etchola through the garden gate.

'I'm not putting up with this much longer!' Daniel was angry. 'We'll have to do something about it!'

Coolly, the cross-eyed man read the name of the villa and then walked back to the main road to study the name of the side-road. He pulled out a note-book and hurriedly scribbled something in it. After this he strolled along the frontage of the Villa Etchola, stopping to peer through the railings every time he had a clear view of the house or the garden.

'I'm beginning to wonder if we haven't made a big mistake by taking refuge in your house,' Steve murmured, embarrassed.

'At least you've nothing to fear while you're with us. Early tomorrow morning, we'll send your father another telegram, as we said, telling him you're at Chiberta. Then all we have to do is wait. Afterwards he should be able to hush it all up.'

'Maybe it'll be too late by then, and the police and the reporters will have already stormed the villa.'

'What makes you think that?'

Steve blushed and looked away.

'First of all, we haven't been able to get rid of that snooper – here he is. And then there's something I just read in the paper. I didn't dare show it to you. Take a look at this, and you'll soon see why the cross-eyed man stands guard outside the Villa Etchola.'

He handed Daniel the paper which Madame Bégou had left in the kitchen. Daniel's eyes widened in surprise as he read the headline:

JACKSON-VILLARS' REWARD NOW REACHES FIFTY THOUSAND

Paris: 15 July. Despite a full-scale police search there is still no sign of Steve and Benny Jackson-Villars. Nor do the two detective agencies involved seem any further forward. Yesterday evening the S.A.M. Bureau revealed that its agents had picked up an important clue on the Italian Riviera. This has now proved false. Meanwhile Interpol-Investigation has been without news of its top man, ex-Superintendent Barboton, for the last two days. None the less the firm makes it plain that they believe their ace-investigator has a lead in the case and that startling developments may be expected shortly. Must we, however, attribute all these delays to sordidly mercenary motives? The reward of twenty thousand francs offered on Thursday last by Monsieur Jackson-Villars, it will be remembered, increases at the rate of five thousand francs a day. Thus one can well imagine that an experienced and patient operator on the trail of the runaways will be in no hurry to disclose the secret. This would be to kill the goose that lays the golden eggs! This is why Steve and Benny are now worth fifty thousand to the lucky winner of this crazy game of hide-and-seek...

Daniel laughed.

'We'll fix that cross-eyed snooper!' he cried. 'It must be that fellow Barboton the paper was talking about. Can you beat it? He took jolly good care to keep his hands off us – the reward wasn't big enough for him two or three days ago!'

'What was so lucky for him was realizing his mistake when we met one another in Bordeaux yesterday!' Steve was furious. 'Now he hasn't got two unimportant doubles, he's got the real Jackson-Villars bottled up in the Villa Etchola at his mercy.'

'Don't you worry. He's bound to have noticed we're on our own here, and I'll bet you he's planning to earn a few thousands more, without lifting his little finger for it. He thinks the reward's in the bag – but we'll take it away from under his very nose! I'm not going to send that telegram tomorrow morning, I'm going to send it now. I'm going to ask your parents to come at once and to come alone. Once your father has my message, nobody else can say they found you.'

'And you'll get the fifty thousand!'

'I hadn't thought of that,' said Daniel. 'Of course I wouldn't dream of taking the reward. The important thing's been all the fun we've had in the last day. I just wanted to help you, that's all.'

'Don't be fussy,' Steve sneered. 'If you don't take it, the cross-eyed man could push his claim. Take it while you've got the chance. Anyway, Daddy won't miss fifty thousand!'

'Well, this is what we'll do,' Daniel decided. 'You stay here and keep an eye on the kids. Don't worry about being seen by that cross-eyed idiot. I'll go indoors right away and phone that telegram. It'll be on its way in five minutes. Then we'll be all prepared.'

The afternoon was spent in cheerful games. Manou and Benny, with Patapon at their heels, crawled through the shrubs and bobbed up by the railings behind the bearded Barboton with piercing yells.

The latter, growing more and more annoyed, muttered into his beard and moved on. Every so often he went off for a little run, returning ten minutes later, the engine on his cycle labouring. The motor no longer ran smoothly, there was a rough note in its whine and it came in sudden bursts, disturbing the neighbourhood like a pneumatic drill. Daniel and Steve kept watch from their vantage-point on the terrace, checking the passengers of every car that went past and eagerly scanning the bend at the end of the road round which the rest of the family might sweep at any moment. There had been no news. The phone had rung only once and that had been the post office asking Daniel to confirm the text of the telegram.

At last, at about five o'clock, just as the garden was growing gold in the evening sunlight, a taxi turned off the Cinq-Cantons road. It was moving very slowly as the driver stuck his head out of the window to read the names of the houses. In the back sat a sunburnt man in a linen suit, calmly smoking his pipe, his broad back resting on a mound of luggage and tin trunks. The taxi made a U-turn and pulled up outside the Villa Etchola.

'Uncle Jérôme!' Daniel yelled, and flew like a madman down the steps of the terrace.

Manou was lurking by the garden gate with Benny. He rushed to open it and flung himself into the traveller's arms.

'I'm a day late,' said Uncle Jérôme as he greeted Daniel in his turn. 'This wretched rail strike held me up. I used it as an excuse to spend a day with friends in Bordeaux. . . . But what's happened to the others?'

'Everybody's late!' Daniel chuckled. 'Grandfather's "movement orders" have gone wrong from beginning to end!'

'What's this? . . . You're on your own here?' Jérôme Quint gasped. 'How long have you been here? And who are these boys anyway?'

He pointed to Steve and Benny standing shyly in the background. Then Daniel told him of all their adventures, not forgetting the part the Jackson-Villars had played at the end.

'You couldn't have been more sensible,' Uncle Jérôme said approvingly when the story was finished. He smiled at the four boys standing in a row in front of him. 'Now we'd better do something about that cross-eyed snooper. What do you say to that? It seems the most urgent thing to me'.

Uncle Jérôme was the practical joker of the family, and the chronicles of the Quints were full of his escapades. With keen interest the burly adult and the four boys leaned over the balustrade of the terrace to see where the snooper was. Barboton had taken good care to get out of the way when a stranger arrived at the villa, but now he was coolly back at his vantage-point in the shade of a tamarisk beside the railings.

'That fellow's a pretty good detective,' Uncle Jérôme muttered. 'You can tell by the way he followed your trail for so long, despite all the different methods of transport you used. He's no less good at his job for having made a mistake about your identity in the first place, and it makes no odds that he only got on to your tracks because he trusted an over-imaginative reporter. But at the same time, he really is – and the one doesn't rule out the other – a blithering idiot! The splendid way he sticks to his post outside the villa shows that he's so greedy for the reward he's nearly out of his mind at the thought of it. Well my lads, it's a very hard job to convince idiots of his sort just by using sweet reason. There's only one sure way of getting rid of them and that's by firing off a gun right behind them . . .'

'And is that what you're going to do, Uncle Jérôme?' asked little Manou, trembling with excitement.

'Just that – and right away!' Uncle Jérôme gave a rumbling laugh. 'As usual, I've brought my favourite guns back on leave with me, and we'll try the biggest – my elephant gun. Come with me!'

Their shoulders shaking with suppressed laughter, the boys followed him indoors. Jérôme Quint took from its case a heavy, black weapon. Just to look at it made you wonder. With a pair of pliers he removed the bullets from two brass-bound cartridges and poured the contents of one into the other.

'Charge super!' He winked. 'This shot's going to cost me fifteen francs in ammunition alone, but I promise you they'll hear it in Biarritz!'

He tamped the cartridge with a piece of wadding, slipped it into the breach and clicked the gun shut. Making sure the safety-catch was on, he set the gun butt to the floor and stuffed almost the whole of a large packet of cotton-wool down the barrel.

'That's it!' he said, picking up the gun and carrying it across his right arm. 'Keep a few yards behind me and don't make a noise.'

The cross-eyed man was still sitting under his tamarisk tree with his back against the railings of the villa and looking disgustedly at the power-cycle in front of him on the pavement. Jérôme Quint bent double, and pushed aside the feathery leaves to stick his head through the railings just above the snooper.

'How long do you mean to hold up the railings of our property?' he asked, most politely.

The cross-eyed man did not move a muscle at the sound of this voice from the clouds. He scratched his ear, looked left and right and, with a show of coolness, began to whistle.

'Hey! It's you I'm talking to!' Uncle Jérôme gave a sudden bellow of rage. 'Are you going to push off, or aren't you?'

Slowly the cross-eyed man looked up. He did not seem in the least surprised by the angry face glaring at him from the bushes.

'Eh, did you say something?' His voice was also loud and he rubbed his forehead. 'I'm a little hard of hearing in the right ear.'

Jérôme Quint's head withdrew, only to reappear on the fellow's left.

'Will you be kind enough to go and sit on somebody else's front door-step: we've had enough of you!' he yelled. 'Did you hear that?'

'Not all of it.'

'What about this then?' And Uncle Jérôme let off the gun right behind his ear.

Barboton leaped like a jack-in-the-box as sparks dropped in a cloud around him. He threw himself on to his pneumatic-drill of a power-cycle, nearly fell off, just managed to right himself and roared down the road, his engine shattering the delightful peace of Chiberta for the next ten minutes. The children rolled on the lawn, laughing until they cried. With great deliberation, Uncle Jérôme opened his gun and carefully blew into the breach to clear the smoke.

'It never fails,' he said calmly. 'You won't see that cross-eyed man again, so you can sleep secure.'

A little later Madame Bégou came over to get their dinner ready. She was very pleased to see her little family increased by one large gentleman in shorts who turned cartwheels and walked on his hands across the lawn.

'Delay the meal, if you can,' Jérôme Quint asked her. 'You never know. . . . Perhaps at the very last minute . . .'

Every time they heard a car stop in the neighbourhood,

Daniel and Manou raced to the gate, and every time they came back disappointed. Their hearts fluttered with the secret knowledge that someone was on the way. As at lunch, Madame Bégou laid a table on the terrace in the open air and the scent of the pines.

They were just starting their soup at eight o'clock, when another taxi drew up outside the villa.

'Here's the third instalment,' Jérôme Quint exclaimed cheerfully as he swept along the terrace in a torrent of nephews and Jackson-Villars. 'Who's it going to be this time? Mother and Father? Jules and his brood? Or Pascal and his wife?'

In fact it was the last who disembarked from the taxi, obviously delighted to be safe in harbour at last; Pascal Quint, tall, spare-faced, blue-eyed and full of vigour despite the touch of grey at the temples; and Lucy Quint, radiating calm and beauty, with the same fair hair and peaches-and-cream complexion which made Manou such a picture. At first sight they seemed surprised to find the villa without its lord and master and to see four children instead of two, four children, moreover, who had such a peculiarly close resemblance to one another. A good fifteen minutes were spent in mutual greetings and in general confusion, made worse by the fact that Manou would insist on everybody saying hullo to Patapon.

'What have you been up to since Easter?' Pascal Quint asked Daniel. 'Your last report wasn't too brilliant.'

'I've just won fifty thousand francs!' Daniel retorted, unconcerned. 'It's as good as in my pocket.'

Grandfather's and Granny's absence had to be explained, as well as the presence of the two strange boys lurking shyly in the background. Pascal Quint grew really angry when he learned, in all its detail, the way in which the family reunion had actually come about, and the fatal part played by the 'movement orders' distributed by old Monsieur Quint. However he gradually calmed down when he realized how well Daniel had handled the situation by himself, with good sense and energy. The obvious good health of Manou, the pet of the family, was proof enough of the care which had been taken of him.

'You mustn't blame Grandfather,' Daniel pleaded. 'It just needed a bit of bad-luck to make things go so wrong. And don't forget he must have been dreadfully worried about Uncle Jules.... The letter he mentioned in his telegram to you at the Hotel Régina, arrived the day before yesterday, and there's a whole lot of stuff that's been forwarded here.'

Pascal Quint discovered among them his own letter sent from England to explain his change of plan, together with one from Monsieur Quint, posted in Saint-Raphaël and dated 12 July. Fortunately it contained the best of news. Jules Quint and his wife were up and about once more, and their children had only been slightly bruised. But they had all had a lucky escape! They had been hit by someone driving much too fast and overtaking on a blind corner, and their car and caravan had crashed into a little ravine on the Esterel near the Auberge des Adrets. Jules Quint had broken his right arm and his wife, Elvisa, had cut her face and badly bruised her left hand. However, if the injured were fit enough to travel they all planned to return to Chiberta by 15 July at the latest, under the wing of the head of the family himself.

'They'll be here tomorow,' exclaimed Lucy Quint, who was very fond of her in-laws. 'And for heaven's sake don't spoil things for Grandfather when he comes. If he finds out about the children, he'll have fifty fits. We'll have to get together to cook up a story for him. It should be easy enough.'

'All right,' said her husband. 'We won't breathe a word about our trip to London, either.'

Lucy Quint left Daniel and Manou for the moment to put her arms around Steve and Benny, as if to warn her husband not to be too hard on them.

'We've still got this big brown envelope Grandfather gave me for you,' Daniel said to his father. 'I opened it in the hope of finding some money inside.'

Curiously, Pascal Quint examined what it contained. The sight of the 'movement orders' drawn up in the smallest detail, drew a fresh howl of rage from him and he tore them in pieces. But the discovery of the cheque soothed his irritation.

'I don't need it, but Father always did worry about every little thing....'

There remained a heap of unimportant old letters. Jérôme chuckled as he read them over his brother's shoulder. Conversation then came back to the Jackson-Villars and the two men began a furious argument about the reward.

'What's all this nonsense about anyway?' Pascal grumbled. 'Of course Daniel won't touch a penny of it.'

'Those fifty thousand francs belong to him!' roared Jérôme. 'It would be crazy to let the cross-eyed man get away with it, after he's made their lives a misery and especially after I've gone out of my way to blast him off the premises!'

'What are you going to do about it?' Pascal Quint turned to his son. 'Invest the money and draw your six per cent?'

Daniel had foreseen the question.

'In all our travels,' he said quietly, 'there was only one man who really helped us whole-heartedly just when we needed it most, and he was the only one who suffered from having met us. I mean the old lorry-driver from the Place Beaubourg – Monsieur Peyrol. Because of us he lost everything. If you'll let me, I'd like to give him the fifty thousand francs.'

Pascal Quint smiled and nodded his consent. He turned to the Jackson-Villars boys and ruffled little Benny's fair hair.

'So it looks as though your parents will be here tomorrow morning,' he said to Steve.

'We hope so,' Daniel answered for him. 'My telegram should be in Monsieur Jackson-Villars' hands by now.'

'Hurrah!' Jérôme shouted, with a great laugh. 'It looks like being a busy day, then. But none of us will worry, the family thrives on upheavals. Monsieur Jackson-Villars may be a seasoned traveller, but I'll bet my last franc that Grandfather won't let him leave the place without a six-page "movement order" for his next urgent business trip to Cincinatti or wherever!'

11

Happy Days

FROM six o'clock onwards, as the rising sun flamed through the pines, the Villa Etchola resounded to the hubbub of running feet, shouting voices, furniture being moved, water splashing and crockery breaking. Pascal and Jérôme Quint had become boys again and they seized possession of the large and unknown house, determined to get the best out of it. A little later, after being tumbled out of bed, the boys raced through the place in their pyjamas pursued by the two brothers armed with sixty feet of garden hose. Poor little Patapon was so drenched that he took refuge of his own free will in the bird-cage on the lawn and chirruped with fright in the midst of the uproar.

An open-air breakfast on the terrace temporarily quietened them. The conversation turned on the absent members of the family.

'I've just rung the station,' Jérôme Quint announced. 'The Ventimiglia-Irun express gets in to Bayonne at about nine o'clock. It's only running half an hour later than normal.'

'We'll both go,' Pascal decided. 'That'll be quite enough. If any more of us come we'll only get into a frightful muddle. Lucy can arrange the official welcome – everybody in line, flowers in hand, smiles on faces.... But do be careful: don't breathe a word about what happened to the kids.... And you boys, keep quiet.... You heard what I said, Manou?'

The telephone in the hall shrilled. It was the post

office at Cinq-Cantons with an urgent telegram for Daniel:

ORLY AIRPORT: FLYING PARIS–BIARRITZ – ARRIVING 10 A.M. – HOPE STEVE BENNY WELL – WARMEST THANKS – JACKSON-VILLARS.

'I told you so!' Jérôme Quint was triumphant. 'We'll get back from the station just in time to dash off to the airport at Parme. . . . In a few hours' time this brand-new villa is going to collapse under all this excitement. Drink up your coffee, Pascal, and let's get off to Bayonne. We mustn't miss the train. Father and Mother'll never be able to manage with two invalids, two babies and the mountains of luggage they must be bringing with them.'

Soon afterwards a taxi bore them off, but their departure did not appreciably lower the fever which by now seized the guests of the Villa Etchola. Steve walked up and down by himself, shoulders nervously hunched, jumping every time a car turned off the main road.

'Don't get so worked up!' Daniel put a kindly arm round his shoulder. 'You told me you only see your parents once in two or three years, and then they're never together. Well, thanks to your little effort, you'll see them together at last. And maybe they will stay like that. So what are you worrying about?'

Steve managed a feeble grin, but his heart was not behind it. Meanwhile, shears in hand, Lucy Quint was snipping all the best flowers which Manou and Benny were tying into pretty bunches. Helped by her grown-up daughter, Madame Bégou bustled to and fro between the two villas carrying baskets of food, cases of bottles and enough bread for a regiment. Daniel kept dashing indoors to look at the clock in the hall. He was beginning to really enjoy his newly-won freedom. From the evening before, the holidays had regained that feeling of something very special and exciting which makes the summer such fun.

The clock struck nine, and Madame Quint sent them all upstairs to change. This was easy, since Daniel's and Manou's clothes fitted Steve and Benny perfectly. The bunches of flowers were hurriedly handed out, and Manou was given, as a special favour, a piece of pink ribbon to tie round Patapon's neck. None of them could keep still. Daniel, at the garden gate, thought that every tradesman's van was the taxi from the station.

Then came the shout of 'Here they are!' and up rolled the three taxis needed to bring the six travellers and their two attendants safely home. The official welcome was taken quite by surprise – the taxis had come along the Cinq-Cantons road instead of the expected way – but it only took a moment to turn round and the Quint family reunion was complete. It was absolute bedlam, with the children laughing and handing their bunches of flowers to whoever they saw first, jumping up and down like young puppies to get a hug and a kiss from everyone. Grandfather had been the first to emerge from the taxis, wearing a grey alpaca suit and a light straw hat. He moved with deliberate slowness, his keen eyes missing nothing. Unbowed by age, he inspected his estate with proprietorial air, saw that everything was in good order and smiled.

'Madame Bégou is a perfect gem of a caretaker.'

Granny, plump and less masterful than her husband, wore a smart summer dress. The first thing she did was to fling herself into the arms of her daughter-in-law to hide the tears of joy which filled her eyes at this happy homecoming. Everybody bustled around the invalids. There was only a small piece of strapping on Aunt Elvisa's hand and two slight scratches showed red on her warm brown cheeks.

'It was nothing to worry about,' she announced with a

grin. 'I pushed my head through the windscreen, that's all!'

Jules Quint was a smaller version of his elder brothers. Pale-faced and slender, and with a friendly, trusting look about him, he stepped out of the taxi cursing the plaster which encased his arm from wrist to elbow.

'I'm going to get rid of this soon, or it'll drive me mad!'

The two brown, chubby babies, Ettore and Francisco, tumbled on to the sandy path with screams of laughter. Manou had climbed up on a garden table to be on a level with all the hugging and kissing that was going on. Old Monsieur Quint greeted Daniel fondly and then rounded on Pascal and Jérôme.

'I know how you laugh behind my back at my written instructions and all the trouble I take to arrange things in advance,' he exclaimed, 'but where would you have been without my "movement orders" in all the chaos of the last few days? Eh? I know that Jules and his family had bad luck, but everything went like clockwork for Pascal and his. There wasn't the slightest risk of these two lads being deserted in the middle of Paris . . . they met Lucy and you at the station all right, as I told them, eh?'

'They were there.' Pascal swallowed hard before replying. 'We managed to hop on the last train from Le Havre . . .'

'And what about the flowers for your mother?' Monsieur Quint turned a grave face towards Daniel.

'The roses at the station weren't good enough,' his grandson answered with complete confidence, 'so we bought a lovely bunch of Parma violets . . . didn't we Manou?'

'Splendid, splendid. In spite of the strike you managed that side of the business all right. So don't you laugh in future when I try to hammer into you my guiding principles – order, method, or-gan-iz-ation! When things go wrong nothing is better than a set of my "movement orders" . . . is it, Daniel?'

'Of course not, Grandfather,' Daniel eagerly agreed. 'Thanks to you, we had a simply splendid time!'

He really did mean what he said. Enough time had elapsed for the memory of the unpleasant moments to fade, and he remembered only the fun he had had.

Jérôme Quint put a friendly arm round his brother's shoulders.

'Poor old Jules, what's happened to your car?'

'Smashed to bits! And the caravan too. It's a bit hard, we only used it for one night.'

'Just how did it happen?'

'It was on a fairly steep hill. I'd just come round a corner, when there was this lunatic right behind. The car skidded, went over the bank and dropped about thirty feet with the caravan behind. Luckily we landed right way up in a little meadow half-way down the hillside.'

Manou opened his mouth and nearly said, 'Just like us!', but he caught Daniel's eye in time.

Then Grandfather noticed the Jackson-Villars boys in the background.

'Who the devil are those two boys?' he asked in surprise. 'I don't think I know them, do I?'

'Oh, they're school-friends of Daniel's,' said Pascal Quint. 'They were caught by the strike in the Hotel Régina, and as they were by themselves the only thing we could do was bring them with us. Their parents are due any minute now to collect them. . . . Anyway, it's time we were going to the airport.'

The two brothers jumped into one of the taxis and were borne off towards Biarritz.

'Plenty of people around!' old Monsieur Quint growled, raising his bushy white eyebrows. 'Place is so new, I'll be losing myself in it next. . . . Where are those

two lads? . . . Ha! The younger one's the spitting image of little Manou. . . . Good morning, boys!'

Daniel introduced them, slurring the name of Jackson-Villars as best he could. Monsieur Quint was completely unaware of its significance. The accident had interrupted his habit of reading a daily newspaper, and in fact he had hardly glanced at one during the past week. He made much of Steve and Benny, having decided that they fitted into the framework of the Villa Etchola very nicely indeed.

'You haven't said hullo to Patapon,' Manou said somewhat crossly, holding up the gentle creature.

'All right, all right!' his grandfather grumbled. 'Hullo, you ugly little brute!'

Then, he tossed Manou into the air, laughing as he caught the little boy of whom he was so fond.

'How I wish I could have seen you waiting on the platform with that lovely bunch of flowers,' he sighed. 'Tell me, was Mummy pleased, really pleased?'

The little boy did not say anything; he merely nodded his head energetically several times and then hid his confusion in his grandfather's shoulder. But it wasn't so very big a sin to have told this small lie. It was better than upsetting a good old man who cared so very much for his family. How could you blame him for wanting to arrange a family reunion as a celebration of his long life and his happy marriage, or for having taken such care to plan in the tiniest detail what his three sons referred to among themselves as the Chiberta Rally?

'Cats ahoy!' Manou gave a sudden and indignant yell over his grandfather's shoulder. 'Hoy! Hoy! Hoy!'

This was the time-honoured warning. Two large tom-cats had slipped over the wall from the villa next door and were creeping through the shrubbery to menace the life of Patapon.

Monsieur Quint waved his walking-stick like a sword and urged the four boys on to chase the cats through the bushes, beating and banging the branches. Everything else stopped as the ladies joined in the fun, Madame Bégou herself aiming the nozzle of the garden hose at the gateway in order to cut off the murderers' retreat.

Monsieur and Madame Jackson-Villars, escorted by the Quint brothers, arrived as the hunt swept through the garden of the Villa Etchola. Jérôme guessed at once what was going on and abandoned the new-comers.

'Watch this! I'm going to get a gun. This will be fun . . .' And he dashed indoors.

Steve and Benny were a little way away from the others. The elder boy was enjoying the sport which made him forget his worries for a while. They crouched as they moved forward, leaping like wild Indians into the bushes.

'I've got one!' Steve shouted. 'Going left! He's all yours, Benny! Don't miss him!'

The cat shot between their legs and as they turned the boys found themselves face to face with the two grown-ups who had crept round behind them along a circular path. Too happy to speak, little Benny raced to his mother. Steve remained still, hanging his head. He knew he had done wrong, but hoped that he had not been as bad as all that. His father made the first approach.

'Come on,' he said, smiling encouragingly. 'If you give me a stick, I'll help you chase the old tom that annoys your friends so much.'

Daniel was watching from the other end of the garden and noticed that all seemed to be going well. Suddenly a terrific explosion shook the house. Stiff with fright, the two cats darted out of a flower-bed and flew towards the garden gate. A stinging jet of hose-water caught them on the way past and they vanished in an appalling series of caterwauls. Uncle Jérôme came round a corner of the terrace, stripped to the waist and carrying a gun.

'Did you see that shot?' he called proudly. 'I peppered their tails for them, believe me! At the rate they were going they'll be back in Bayonne by now!'

Exhausted with laughter, the beaters congratulated one another on their efforts.

'As long as Patapon is at the Villa Etchola, no cat will be allowed to cross the threshold!' Grandfather boomed. 'And I mean that . . .'

'You can't be serious,' old Madame Quint said with a laugh. She had stood and watched from the front door. 'I'd never have believed it. The first thing you all do when you get out of the train is to join in the slaughter of two innocent pussy-cats. Come and sit down for a moment.'

Madame Bégou had set out deck-chairs and garden seats on the lawn in the shade of the pine-trees. The master of the house was the first to sit down and demand a drink. Then, passing from one mood to another, his eyes began to sparkle as he observed Monsieur and Madame Jackson-Villars strolling towards the house with their arms round Steve and Benny.

'Who the devil are those people?' he burst out. 'Do they think the place is a public park? How long have people been able to turn the Villa Etchola into Liberty Hall?'

'They're the friends I was telling you about a moment ago,' said Pascal Quint. 'We brought them back from the airport while you were busy hunting cats.'

'Good, good, good! Better stay to lunch, then,' Grandfather decided, passing as rapidly from storm to calm.

'But where have I seen that woman before . . . she's a good-looker!'

Ten years before, Madame Jackson-Villars had been a leading film-star of recognized talent. Her slim figure, blond hair and lovely face still preserved traces of her earlier beauty. Her tall sunburnt husband beside her was a typical businessman so absorbed in his activities that he was quite unused to the idea of taking an hour off for the simple pleasure of living. That morning all seemed changed. The smile on their lips reflected something more than mere self-satisfaction or pride in their status as millionaires. In their children's company they had rediscovered a pleasure they had long despised, a pleasure that rates nothing in the day of a society woman or in the balance-sheet of a financier. It was easy for Steve to guess what had happened and he thought he had succeeded.

Pascal Quint introduced them to everyone. He must have coached them in the version of recent events for his father's ear, for they never once tripped up in conversation. Nonetheless, the barriers were very soon down.

'I hadn't seen Benny for six months, nor Steve for a whole year,' Monsieur Jackson-Villars confessed with a shake of his head. 'The life I lead is quite impossible.'

'I was nearly the same,' Pascal Quint admitted. 'Luckily my wanderings will be over in a few months' time. I don't want to wreck my life for the sake of my job. My sons need me around.'

Grandfather, naughtily, pretended to be unconcerned by all these problems. He turned abruptly to his favourite.

'Come here, Manou, and show Patapon to Monsieur Jackson-Villars.'

Manou introduced the guinea-pig, nestling in the hollow of his left shoulder.

'Say hullo to him,' he told the millionaire solemnly, 'or Grandfather won't ask you to lunch.'

The party gradually split up into congenial groups. On the pretext of showing their guest the house, Pascal managed to take Monsieur Jackson-Villars aside to give him a detailed account of the boys' adventures. Daniel followed at their heels, happy and proud to be able to prompt his father while things were still fresh in his mind. At the right moment he produced the paper which had caused their wild flight.

'Monsieur Kern, our lawyer, is just as much to blame as I am,' the millionaire protested. 'He'd only met Steve once or twice, and he let himself be taken in by that extraordinary likeness between my Benny and your Manou. In the silly season the papers get hold of anything, and the *Europe-Soir* were fools enough to print a photo which should never have been developed in the first place.'

Daniel had not been following without a purpose, and now he began to feel things were moving in his favour.

'Incidentally,' Monsieur Jackson-Villars suddenly said to him, 'half an hour after I'd got your telegram last night, I had another from somebody called Barboton, on behalf of Interpol-Investigation. I shouldn't have taken any notice of it in any case – the message you sent from Bordeaux had set my mind at rest. . . . Here's the cheque,' he added with a smile. 'Signed it myself. It's worth fifty thousand.'

Daniel paused and looked at his father.

'Take it,' Monsieur Jackson-Villars went on. 'If it hadn't been for you this whole sorry business would have ended tragically, I'm sure. Public opinion isn't too kind to people in my privileged position. . . . So take it!'

Daniel took the cheque with a gesture of childish pleasure. Monsieur Peyrol would have his new lorry now! The millionaire rested his hands on Daniel's shoulders and looked into his face.

'And now my boy, will you tell me, man to man, whether you think Steve was right to do what he did?'

'No,' Daniel replied, unprompted. 'I think children have better ways of making their protest just as strongly. It was bad luck Steve chose the worst way he possibly could. You can blame his Irish blood. It makes him do things on the spur of the moment.'

'I've forgiven him for everything already.' Monsieur Jackson-Villars sighed. 'Even for having dragged poor little Benny off on his crazy adventure.'

'That was the best thing for him,' Daniel murmured. 'I know what I'm talking about, because I went through the same thing myself. . . . Steve now understands the anxiety you can feel for somebody smaller than you who relies on you.'

Pascal Quint gave his son an odd look. It was not hard to realize what Daniel meant. The blow went home to Monsieur Jackson-Villars and he looked away. Just then, his wife came up hand-in-hand with Steve and Benny. She heard the last sentence, and although it was only a boy who spoke, what he said explained the past and arranged the future. These blunt words set parents and children in their places, together in the warmth of a real family life.

Pascal Quint tried to dispel the embarrassed silence of his guests.

'I'm not so sure that Daniel and Manou aren't the winners of our Chiberta Rally,' he told them cheerfully. 'But why don't *you* stay on here for a few days?'

Madame Jackson-Villars looked at her husband.

'Chiberta really is a charming spot.' She smiled. 'We've made up our minds. We're going to spend a long and happy holiday here with our children.'

Five minutes before lunch was due, Madame Bégou noticed to her annoyance that the champagne had been forgotten. She told Granny, who at once warned Monsieur Quint.

'Take the Bégou girl's bicycle,' Grandfather told Daniel, 'and fetch three bottles from old Madame Irigoyen on the corner of the Rue d'Anglet.'

'Right,' said the delighted Daniel. 'Where is it?'

'Take the first turning on the right and follow the sea-front until you get to the swimming-pool. Then take the turning on the left. . . .'

He stopped suddenly and took his pen and notebook out of his pocket. He gazed gravely at Daniel over the rims of his glasses.

'I'll write you out a "Movement order",' he said with a sniff of pleasure. 'That'll be much the simplest thing.'

'No!' his three sons yelled with one voice, raising imploring arms to heaven.

And Daniel was well on his way.

About the Author

Paul Berna was born at Hyeres in 1913. He was the youngest son of a large, noisy and quarrelsome family where everybody had a good deal of fun. He spent the whole of his childhood in the South of France, and though circumstances have forced him to spend a lot of time elsewhere he has always been very attached to this part of the country.

He went to school in Toulon and later at Aix, where he did very well passing his pre-university exam with credit. His great interest in books and literature of every kind went hand in hand with an enthusiasm for football and swimming. After leaving school he did a two year apprenticeship at a Paris bank. This was followed by a number of jobs, none of which really appealed to him. After the Second World War he was offered an administrative job in the Post Office.

In spite of his professional occupations he has always been interested in young people and their books. Indeed, all his works show that he has a remarkable insight into the mind of the modern child.

A Hundred Million Francs, *The Street Musician*, *The Knights of King Midas* and *Flood Warning* are all available in Puffins.

In 1960 he married Saint-Marcoux who is well known for her novels for older girls.

SOME OTHER PUFFINS

Danny Dunn on a Desert Island

Jay Williams & Raymond Abrashkin

'Euclid Bullfinch,' said Dr Grimes, 'I challenge you to a duel of desert islands. I will go ashore on one island, and you on another, and we'll see which of us makes himself more comfortable.'

'Oh, boy!' whispered Danny Dunn, and made up his mind to be in on the adventure – though even he could never have guessed how desperately exciting and dangerous it was all going to be.

The Case of the Silver Egg

Desmond Skirrow

'Quick,' said Fatty Sharp to the taxi driver. 'Follow that car and it's double the fare.'

The boys piled into the cab. There were only five of of them, but to the cab-driver it must have seemed as though half the small boys in South London were swarming into his vehicle.

The chase really was a matter of life and death. For Mini-Minor Morris's father the Professor was a prisoner in the car, kidnapped with his brilliant discovery the Silver Egg, the greatest source of industrial energy known to man. And Mini himself, the boys' intrepid and scientifically-minded leader, was shut in the boot. (This lively story has now been filmed for television under the title *The Queen Street Gang*.)

My Side of the Mountain

Jean George

'I am on my mountain in a tree home that people have passed without ever knowing I am here. The house is a hemlock tree six feet in diameter. I came upon it last summer and dug and burnt it out until I made a snug home in the tree.

My bed is on the right, on the left is a small fireplace with a chimney that leads the smoke out through a knothole. It snowed all day yesterday and today. It must be below zero outside, and yet I can sit here inside my tree and write with bare hands. It is the fourth of December, I think. It is eight months since I ran away from home.'

This is part of Sam Gribley's diary. Sam had escaped from his family's cramped flat in New York and his eight brothers and sisters to live on the barren farm his grandfather had owned in the Catskill Mountains. He had a pen-knife, an axe, a ball of string, and some flint and steel, and that was all.

Run For Your Life

David Line

'I want to report a murder,' Soldier said.
'Where?'
'I don't know where,' Soldier said.
'Who's been murdered?'
'Nobody yet,' Soldier said. 'That's what I want to tell you.'

Nobody said anything while he got it out. The other policemen stopped what they were doing and listened, but none believed Soldier had really overheard the men planning a murder.

But the men did commit the murder, and they knew only one way to stop the boys telling what they had seen . . .

This was David Line's first suspense story for children, and it was serialised on television as *Soldier and Me*.